POCKET HOLT HANDBOOK

LAURIE G. KIRSZNER
University of the
Sciences in Philadelphia

STEPHEN R. MANDELL
Drexel University

HARCOURT BRACE COLLEGE PUBLISHERS

FORT WORTH   PHILADELPHIA   SAN DIEGO   NEW YORK
ORLANDO   AUSTIN   SAN ANTONIO
TORONTO   MONTREAL   LONDON   SYDNEY   TOKYO

Publisher: Earl McPeek
Acquisitions Editor: Julie McBurney
Developmental Editor: Camille Adkins
Market Strategist: John Meyers
Project Editor: Denise Netardus
Art Director: Garry Harman
Production Manager: Linda McMillan

ISBN: 0-15-507239-0
Library of Congress Catalog Card Number: 99-60264

Address for orders:
Harcourt, Inc., 6277 Sea Harbor Drive, Orlando, FL
32887-6777
1-800-782-4479

Address for international orders:
International Customer Service
Harcourt, Inc., 6277 Sea Harbor Drive, Orlando, FL
32887-6777
407-345-3800
(fax) 407-345-4060
(E-mail) hbintl@harcourtbrace.com

Address for editorial correspondence:
Harcourt College Publishers, 301 Commerce Street, Suite 3700, Fort Worth, TX 76102

Web site address:
http://www.hbcollege.com

Printed in the United States of America

0 1 2 3 4 5 6 7 8 039 9 8 7 6 5

PREFACE

We would like to introduce you to the first edition of *The* Pocket *Holt Handbook,* a quick reference guide for college students. This book is designed to be a truly portable handbook that will easily fit in a backpack or in a pocket, yet serve as a valuable resource. Despite its compact size, *The* Pocket *Holt Handbook* offers coverage of the writing process; sentence grammar; major sentence errors; ESL; word choice; punctuation and mechanics; research; MLA, APA, CMS, and CBE documentation; and document design—in short, all the topics that you expect to find in a much longer book. Unlike other concise handbooks, *The* Pocket *Holt Handbook* includes examples of writing that can serve as models for college students not just in first-year writing courses, but throughout college and beyond.

In preparing the first edition of *The* Pocket *Holt Handbook,* we concentrated on making the book inviting, useful, clear, and, most of all, easy to navigate. In addition to the book's reduced size, we have incorporated distinctive design features throughout that make information easy to find.

- A color-coded guide to the parts of the book appears on the front cover. Each part of the book is marked by a distinctive color bar that corresponds to a color on this guide.
- A brief contents is provided on the inside front cover.
- Close-up boxes that focus on special problems are identified by a magnifying glass icon.
- Checklists, designed to provide quick reference, are distinguished by a check mark icon.
- Computer boxes highlight information that students will use as they write and revise papers on their computers and are noted by a computer icon.
- Boxed lists and charts set off other information that students are likely to refer to on a regular basis.
- Marginal cross-references (which are keyed to blue, underlined terms in the text) direct readers to related discussions in other parts of the book.

The publication of *The* Pocket *Holt Handbook* completes *The Holt Handbook* series: *The Holt Handbook,* for those who want a full-size, comprehensive reference book with exercises; *The* Brief *Holt Handbook,* for those who want a compact, tabbed reference guide; and now *The* Pocket *Holt Handbook,* for those who want a portable, quick reference. Throughout all these books, our goal was the same: to give students the guidance they need to become self-reliant writers and to succeed in college and beyond.

CONTENTS

Contents

Contents

Contents

PART 1

WRITING ESSAYS AND PARAGRAPHS

CHAPTER 1

WRITING ESSAYS

1a Understanding the Writing Process

Writing is a constant process of decision making—of selecting, deleting, and rearranging material.

THE WRITING PROCESS

Planning: Consider your purpose, audience, and assignment; choose a topic; discover ideas to write about.
Shaping: Decide how to organize your material.
Drafting: Write your first draft.
Revising: "Re-see" what you have written; write additional drafts.
Editing: Check grammar, spelling, punctuation, and mechanics.
Proofreading: Check for typographical errors.

1b Understanding Essay Structure

The essays you write in college will have a thesis-and-support structure. A **thesis-and-support essay** includes a **thesis statement** (which expresses the **thesis,** or main idea, of the essay) and the specific information that explains and develops that thesis. Your essay will consist of several paragraphs—an <u>introductory paragraph</u>, which introduces your thesis; a <u>concluding paragraph</u>, which gives your essay a sense of completion, perhaps restating your thesis; and a number of **body paragraphs,** which support your essay's thesis.

See 2d1
See 2d2

1c Writing Effective Thesis Statements

An effective thesis statement has four characteristics.

1. *An effective thesis statement clearly communicates your essay's main idea.* It tells your readers not only what your

3

essay's topic is, but also how you will approach that topic and what you will say about it. Thus, your thesis statement reflects your essay's purpose.

2. *An effective thesis statement is more than a general subject, a statement of fact, or an announcement of your intent.*

SUBJECT: Intelligence tests

STATEMENT OF FACT: Intelligence tests are used extensively in some elementary schools.

ANNOUNCEMENT: The essay that follows will show that intelligence tests may be inaccurate.

THESIS STATEMENT: Although intelligence tests are widely used for placement in many elementary schools, they are not always the best measure of a student's academic performance.

3. *An effective thesis statement is carefully worded.* Your thesis statement—usually expressed in a single, concise sentence—should be direct and straightforward. Do not use vague, abstract phrases, such as *centers on, deals with, involves, revolves around,* or *is concerned with.* Also avoid overly complex terminology and unnecessary details that might confuse or mislead readers. Finally, do not include phrases like *As I will show, I plan to demonstrate,* and *It seems to me,* which weaken your credibility by suggesting that your conclusions are based on opinion rather than on reading, observation, and experience.

4. *Finally, an effective thesis statement suggests your essay's direction, emphasis, and scope.* Your thesis statement should not make promises that your essay will not fulfill. It should suggest how your ideas are related, in what order your major points will be introduced, and where you will place your emphasis, as the following thesis statement does.

Widely ridiculed as escape reading, romance novels are becoming increasingly important as a proving ground for many first-time writers and, more significantly, as a showcase for strong heroines.

This thesis statement tells readers that the essay to follow will focus on two major roles of the romance novel and that the role of the romance as escapist fiction will be treated briefly. It also indicates the order in which the various ideas will be discussed.

REVISING YOUR THESIS STATEMENT

As you write and rewrite, you may modify your essay's direction, emphasis, and scope; if you do so, you must re-word your thesis statement.

TENTATIVE THESIS STATEMENT (*rough draft*): Professional sports can be corrupted by organized crime.

REVISED THESIS STATEMENT (*final paper*): Although supporters of legalized gambling argue that organized crime cannot influence professional sports, the fixing of the 1919 World Series suggests the opposite.

1d Drafting and Revising

(1) Writing a Rough Draft

A rough draft gets ideas down on paper so you can react to them. You will generally rewrite your essay several times, so you should expect to add or delete words, to reword sentences, to re-think ideas, to reorder paragraphs—and even to take an unex-pected detour that may lead you to a new perspective on your topic. To make revision easier, leave room on the page so that you can add material or rewrite. If you type, triple-space; if you write, skip lines. To streamline your revision process, use sym-bols—arrows, circles, boxes, numbers, and so on—that signal various operations to you.

(2) Revising Your Drafts

 STRATEGIES FOR REVISION

- **Outline your draft.** An outline can help you check the structure of your paper.
- **Do collaborative revision.** Ask a friend to give you feedback on your draft.
- **Use instructors' comments.** Study written comments on your draft, and arrange a conference if necessary.
- **Use revision checklists.** Look at the whole essay, and then consider the paragraphs, sentences, and words.

✔ CHECKLIST: REVISING THE WHOLE ESSAY

- ✔ Are thesis and support logically related, with each body paragraph supporting your thesis statement? **(See 1b)**
- ✔ Is your thesis statement clearly and specifically worded? **(See 1c)**
- ✔ Have you discussed everything promised in your thesis statement? **(See 1c)**

✔ CHECKLIST: REVISING PARAGRAPHS

- ✔ Does each body paragraph focus on one main idea, expressed in a clearly worded topic sentence? **(See 2a)**
- ✔ Are the relationships of sentences within paragraphs clear? **(See 2b)**
- ✔ Are your body paragraphs fully developed? **(See 2c)**
- ✔ Does your introductory paragraph arouse interest and prepare readers for what is to come? **(See 2d1)**
- ✔ Does your concluding paragraph review your main points? **(See 2d2)**

✔ CHECKLIST: REVISING SENTENCES

- ✔ Have you used correct sentence structure? **(See Chs. 3 and 4)**
- ✔ Are your sentences varied? **(See Ch. 9)**
- ✔ Have you eliminated nonessential words and unnecessary repetition? **(See 10a–b)**
- ✔ Have you avoided overloading your sentences with too many clauses? **(See 10c)**
- ✔ Have you avoided potentially confusing shifts in tense, voice, mood, person, or number? **(See 11a)**
- ✔ Are your sentences constructed logically? **(See 11b–c)**
- ✔ Have you strengthened sentences with repetition, balance, and parallelism? **(See 12a)**
- ✔ Have you placed modifiers clearly and logically? **(See Ch. 13)**

Essays 1e

✔ CHECKLIST: REVISING WORDS

✔ Have you eliminated jargon, pretentious diction, clichés, and offensive language from your writing? **(See 14a–d)**

CLOSE-UP CHOOSING A TITLE

- A title should convey your essay's focus, perhaps using key words and phrases from your essay or echoing the wording of your assignment.
- A title should arouse interest, perhaps with a provocative question, a quotation, or a note of controversy.

  ASSIGNMENT: Write about a problem faced on college campuses today.

  TOPIC: Free speech on campus

  POSSIBLE TITLES:
  Free Speech: A Problem for Today's Colleges (descriptive; echoes wording of assignment and includes key words of essay)

  How Free Should Free Speech on Campus Be? (provocative question)

  The Right to "Shout 'Fire' in a Crowded Theater" (quotation)

  Hate Speech: A Dangerous Abuse of Free Speech on Campus (controversial position)

1e Editing and Proofreading

When you **edit,** you concentrate on grammar and spelling, punctuation and mechanics. When you **proofread,** you reread every word carefully to make sure you did not make any errors as you typed.

EDITING AND PROOFREADING

- As you edit, look at only a small portion of text at a time. If your software allows you to split the screen,

continued on the following page

continued from the previous page

create another window so small that you can see only one or two lines of text at a time.

- Use the *search* or *find* command to look for words or phrases in usage errors that you commonly make— for instance, confusing *it's* with *its*. You can also un-cover **sexist language** by searching for words like *he, his, him,* or *man*.
- Remember that a spell checker will not recognize *there* as a mistake when you mean *their* or the mis-spelled *work* when you mean *word*. You still must proofread your papers carefully.

See
14d2

1f Model Student Paper

Masterton 1

Samantha Masterton

Professor Wade

English 101

15 November 1999

Title

The Returning Student:

Older Is Definitely Better

After graduating from high school, young people must decide what they want to do with the rest of their lives. Many graduates (often without much thought) decide to continue their education in college. This group of teenagers makes up what many see as the typical first-year college student. Recently, however, there has been Thesis statement an influx of older students into American colleges and universities. My experience as one of these older students has convinced me that many students would benefit from taking a few years off between high school and college.

First point in support of thesis

Many eighteen-year-olds are not ready for college. Teenagers are often concerned with things other than cracking books--going to parties, dating, and testing personal limits, for example. I almost never see older students cutting lectures or wasting time as younger students do. Most older students have saved for tuition and want to get their money's worth, just as I do. Many are also balancing the demands of home and work to attend classes, so they know how important it is to do well.

Generally, young people just out of high school have not learned how to set priorities or meet deadlines. Younger college students often find themselves hopelessly behind or scrambling at the last minute simply because they have not learned how to budget their time. Although success in college depends on the ability to set realistic goals and organize time and materials, college itself does little to help students develop these skills. On the contrary, the workplace--where reward and punishment are usually immediate and tangible--is the best place to learn such lessons. Working teaches the basics that college takes for granted: the value of punctuality and attendance, the importance of respect for

Second point in support of thesis

superiors and colleagues, and the need for establishing priorities and meeting deadlines.

The adult student who has gained experience in the workplace has advantages over the teenaged student. In general, the older student enrolls in college with a definite course of study in mind. For the adult student, college is an extension of work rather than a place to discover what work will be. This greater sense of purpose makes older students more focused and more highly motivated.

Third point in support of thesis

Fourth point in support of thesis

Because of their age and greater experience, older students bring more into the classroom than younger students do. Eighteen-year-olds have been driving for only a year or two; they have just gotten the right to vote; and they usually have not lived on their own. In contrast, older students have generally had a variety of real-life experiences. This experience enables them to make significant contributions to class discussions and group projects, and it enriches their written work as well. Moreover, their years in the real world have helped them to become more focused and more responsible than they were when they graduated from high school. As a result,

Masterton 4

they are better prepared for college. Thus, they not only bring more into the classroom, but they also take more out of it.

Conclusion

All things considered, higher education is often wasted on the young, who are either too immature or too unfocused to take advantage of it. Many older students have taken time off to serve in the military, to get a job, or to raise a family. Many have traveled, read widely, engaged in informal study, and taken the time to grow up. By the time they get to college, they have defined their goals and made a commitment to achieve them. Taking a few years off between high school and college would give younger students the breathing room they need to make the most of college. It would also give them the life experience they need to appreciate the value of their education.

CHAPTER 2

WRITING PARAGRAPHS

A **paragraph** is a group of related sentences, which may be complete in itself or part of a longer piece of writing.

✓ CHECKLIST: WHEN TO PARAGRAPH

- ✔ Begin a new paragraph whenever you move from one major point to another.
- ✔ Begin a new paragraph whenever you move your readers from one time period or location to another.
- ✔ Begin a new paragraph every time you begin discussing a new step in a process.
- ✔ Begin a new paragraph when you want to emphasize an important idea.
- ✔ Begin a new paragraph every time a new person speaks.
- ✔ Begin a new paragraph to signal the end of your introduction and the beginning of your conclusion.

2a Writing Unified Paragraphs

A paragraph is **unified** when it develops a single idea. Each paragraph should have a **topic sentence** that states the main idea of the paragraph; the other sentences in the paragraph support that idea.

<u>I was a listening child, careful to hear the very different sounds of Spanish and English.</u> Wide-eyed with hearing, I'd listen to sounds more than words. First, there were English (*gringo*) sounds. So many words were still unknown that when the butcher or the lady at the drugstore said something to me, exotic polysyllabic sounds would bloom in the midst of their sentences. Often the speech of people in public seemed to me very loud, booming with confidence. The man behind the counter would literally ask, "What can I do for you?" But by being so firm and so clear, the sound of his voice said that he was a *gringo;* he belonged in public society. (Richard Rodriguez, *Aria: A Memoir of a Bilingual Childhood*)

Topic sentence

Support

2b Writing Coherent Paragraphs

A paragraph is **coherent** when all its sentences are logically related to one another. **Transitional words and phrases** clarify the relationships among sentences by establishing the spatial, chronological, and logical connections within a paragraph.

Topic sentence	Napoleon certainly made a change for the worse by leaving his small kingdom of Elba. <u>After Waterloo,</u> he went back to Paris, and he abdicated for a second time. <u>A hundred days after</u> his return from Elba, he fled to Rochefort in hope of escaping to America. <u>Finally,</u> he gave himself up to the English captain of the ship *Bellerophon*. <u>Once again,</u> he suggested that the Prince Regent grant him asylum, and <u>once again,</u> he was refused. <u>In the end,</u> all he saw of England was the Devon coast and Plymouth Sound as he passed on to the remote island of St. Helena. <u>After six years of exile,</u> he died on May 5, 1821, at the age of fifty-two. (Norman Mackenzie, *The Escape from Elba*)

Transitional words and phrases — after, finally, and so on — establish chronology of events.

USING TRANSITIONAL WORDS AND PHRASES

To Signal Sequence or Addition
again, also, besides, furthermore, in addition, first . . . second . . . third, one . . . another, too

To Signal Time
afterward, as soon as, at first, at the same time, before, earlier, finally, in the meantime, later, meanwhile, next, now, soon, subsequently, then, until

To Signal Comparison
also, by the same token, likewise, in comparison, similarly

To Signal Contrast
although, but, despite, even though, however, in contrast, instead, meanwhile, nevertheless, nonetheless, on the contrary, on the one hand . . . on the other hand, still, whereas, yet

To Signal Examples
for example, for instance, namely, specifically, thus

continued on the following page

continued from the previous page

To Signal Narrowing of Focus
after all, indeed, in fact, in other words, in particular, specifically, that is

To Signal Conclusions or Summaries
as a result, consequently, in summary, therefore, in conclusion, in other words, thus, to conclude

To Signal Concession
admittedly, certainly, granted, naturally, of course

To Signal Causes or Effects
accordingly, as a result, because, consequently, hence, since, so, then, therefore

NOTE: Parallel constructions ("He was a patriot. . . . He was a reformer. . . . He was an innovator. . . .") and repeated key words and phrases ("He invented a new type of printing press. . . . This printing press. . . .") can also help you achieve coherence.

2c Writing Well-Developed Paragraphs

A paragraph is **well developed** when it contains all the support—examples, statistics, expert opinion, and so on—that readers need to understand the main idea.

From Thanksgiving until Christmas, children are bombarded with ads for violent toys and games. Toy manufacturers persist in thinking that only toys that appeal to children's aggressiveness will sell. <u>One television commercial praises the merits of a commando team that attacks and captures a miniature enemy base. Toy soldiers wear realistic uniforms and carry automatic rifles, pistols, knives, grenades, and ammunition. Another commercial shows laughing children shooting one another with plastic rocket fighters and tanklike vehicles.</u> Despite claims that they (unlike action toys) have educational value, video games have increased the level of violence. <u>The most popular video games involve children in strikingly realistic combat situations. One game lets children search out and destroy enemy fighters in outer space. Other bestselling games graphically simulate hand-to-hand combat on city streets.</u> The real question is why parents continue to buy these violent toys for their children. (Student Writer)

Topic sentence

Specific examples

Specific examples

2d **Writing Introductory and Concluding Paragraphs**

(1) Introductory Paragraphs

An **introductory paragraph** introduces the subject, narrows it down, and then states the essay's thesis.

> Christine was just a girl in one of my classes. I never knew much about her except that she was strange. She didn't talk much. Her hair was dyed black and purple, and she always wore heavy black boots and a black turtleneck sweater. She was attractive—in spite of the ring she wore through her left eyebrow—but she never seemed to care what the rest of us thought about her. Like the rest of my classmates, I didn't really want to get close to her. <u>It was only when we were assigned to do our chemistry project together that I began to understand why Christine dressed the way she did.</u> (Student Writer)

Thesis statement

An introductory paragraph may also include an interesting quotation, a compelling question, an unusual comparison, or a controversial statement.

NOTE: Avoid introductions that simply announce your subject ("In my paper I will talk about Lady Macbeth") or that undercut your credibility ("I don't know much about alternative energy sources, but I would like to present my opinion").

> ✔ **CHECKLIST: INTRODUCTORY PARAGRAPHS**
>
> ✔ Does your introduction include your essay's thesis statement?
> ✔ Does it lead naturally into the body of your essay?
> ✔ Does it arouse your readers' interest?
> ✔ Does it avoid statements that simply announce your subject or that undercut your credibility?

(2) Concluding Paragraphs

A **concluding paragraph** typically begins with specifics—for example, a review of the essay's main points—and then moves to more general statements.

> As an Arab-American, I feel I have the best of two worlds. I'm proud to be part of the melting pot, proud to contribute to the tremendous diversity of cultures, customs and traditions that makes this country unique. But Arab-bashing—

public acceptance of hatred and bigotry—is something no American can be proud of. (Ellen Mansoor Collier, "I Am Not a Terrorist")

A concluding paragraph may also offer a prediction, a recommendation, a forceful opinion, or a pertinent quotation.

NOTE: Avoid conclusions that just repeat your introduction in different words or that cast doubt on your concluding points ("I may not be an expert" or "At least this is my opinion"). End with a statement that readers will remember.

✔ CHECKLIST: CONCLUDING PARAGRAPHS

- ✔ Does your conclusion remind readers of the primary focus of your essay?
- ✔ Does it review your essay's main points?
- ✔ Does it do more than just repeat the introduction?
- ✔ Does it avoid apologies?
- ✔ Does it end memorably?

PART 2

WRITING GRAMMATICAL SENTENCES

CHAPTER 3

REVISING COMMA SPLICES AND FUSED SENTENCES

A **comma splice** occurs when two independent clauses are joined by just a comma. A **fused sentence** occurs when two independent clauses are joined with no punctuation.

COMMA SPLICE: Charles Dickens created the character of Mr. Micawber, he also created Uriah Heep.

FUSED SENTENCE: Charles Dickens created the character of Mr. Micawber he also created Uriah Heep.

✔ CHECKLIST: REVISING COMMA SPLICES AND FUSED SENTENCES

To revise a comma splice or fused sentence, use one of the following strategies.

- ✔ Use a period to separate the clauses.
- ✔ Use a semicolon to separate the clauses.
- ✔ Add an appropriate coordinating conjunction.
- ✔ Subordinate one clause to the other.

3a Revising with Periods

You can use a period to separate the independent clauses, creating two separate sentences. This is a good strategy when the clauses are long or when they are not related.

In 1894 Frenchman Alfred Dreyfus was falsely convicted of treason, his struggle for justice pitted the army against the civil libertarians.

3b Revising with Semicolons

You can use a <u>semicolon</u> to separate two closely related clauses that convey parallel or constrasting information.

See
17a

19

Chippendale chairs have straight legs;however,Queen Anne

chairs have curved legs.

COMMA SPLICES AND TRANSITIONAL WORDS

See
2b

When you use a **transitional word or phrase** (such
as *however, therefore,* or *for example*) to connect two independent clauses, the transitional element must be preceded by a semicolon and followed by a comma. If you
use a comma alone, you create a comma splice. If you
omit punctuation entirely, you create a fused sentence.

3c Revising with Coordinating Conjunctions

See
9a1

You can use an appropriate coordinating conjunction (*and,
or, but, nor, for, so, yet*) to create a **compound sentence**. Be sure
to add a comma before the coordinating conjunction.

Elias Howe invented the sewing machine, and Julia Ward Howe

was a poet and social reformer.

3d Revising with Subordinating Conjunctions or Relative Pronouns

When the ideas in two independent clauses are not of equal
importance, use an appropriate subordinating conjunction or
relative pronoun to place the less important idea in a dependent
See
9a2
clause, creating a **complex sentence**.

Stravinsky's ballet *The Rite of Spring* shocked Parisians in
1913, because its rhythms seemed erotic.

Lady Mary Wortley Montagu, who had suffered from smallpox
herself, she helped spread the practice of inoculation.

CHAPTER 4

REVISING SENTENCE FRAGMENTS

A **sentence fragment** occurs when an incomplete sentence —a clause or a phrase—is punctuated as if it were complete. To determine whether a sentence is incomplete, ask these four questions.

1. Does the word group lack a subject?

   Many astrophysicists now believe that galaxies are distributed in clusters. <u>And even form supercluster complexes.</u>

2. Does the word group lack a verb?

   Three key events defined my generation. <u>The Gulf War, the Oklahoma City bombing, and the Rodney King verdict.</u>

3. Does the word group lack both a subject and a verb?

   Researchers are engaged in a variety of studies. <u>Suggesting a link between alcoholism and heredity.</u> (*Suggesting* is a **verbal**, which cannot serve as a sentence's main verb.)

4. Does the word group consist of a dependent clause alone? (A sentence cannot consist of a single clause that begins with a **subordinating conjunction** or with a **relative pronoun**.)

   See 9a2

   Bishop Desmond Tutu was awarded the 1984 Nobel Peace Prize. <u>Because he struggled to end apartheid.</u>

   The pH meter and the spectrophotometer are two scientific instruments. <u>That changed the chemistry laboratory dramatically.</u>

✔ CHECKLIST: REVISING SENTENCE FRAGMENTS

To revise a sentence fragment, use one or more of the following strategies.

✔ Supply the missing subject or verb (or both).
✔ Attach the fragment to a nearby independent clause.
✔ Delete the subordinating conjunction or relative pronoun.

4a Supplying the Missing Subject or Verb

When a fragment lacks a subject or a verb or both, you can correct it by supplying the missing words. For example, if the

See
B2.3

fragment is a **verbal phrase**, you can correct it by substituting a verb for the verbal and adding a subject.

In 1948, India became independent. ~~Divided~~ ^{It was divided} into the nations of India and Pakistan.

A familiar trademark can increase a product's sales. ~~Reminding~~ ^{It reminds} shoppers the product has a longstanding reputation.

CLOSE-UP REVISING SENTENCE FRAGMENTS: LISTS

See
25a1

When a fragment takes the form of a **list**, add a colon to connect the list to the sentence that introduces it.

Tourists often outnumber residents in four European cities : Venice, Florence, Canterbury, and Bath.

4b Attaching the Fragment to an Independent Clause

Often, you can correct a fragment by attaching it to a nearby independent clause to create a complete sentence.

Property taxes rose sharply , although ~~Although~~ city services declined.

See
B2.3

(**dependent clause** fragment)

The battery is dead , which ~~Which~~ means the car won't start. (dependent clause fragment)

President Johnson did not seek reelection , for ~~For~~ a number of

See
B2.3

reasons. (**prepositional phrase** fragment)

Brian was the star forward of the Blue Devils , a ~~A~~ team that

See
7b3

won nearly every game. (**appositive** fragment)

Fairy tales are full of damsels in distress , such ~~Such~~ as Rapunzel.

(appositive fragment)

They took only a compass and a canteen~~. And~~ _x some trail
mix. (part of compound object)

written above "And": and

4c Deleting the Subordinating Conjunction or Relative Pronoun

When a fragment consists of a dependent clause that is
punctuated as if it were a complete sentence, you can correct it
by attaching it to an adjacent independent clause, as illustrated
in **4b.** Alternatively, you can simply delete the subordinating
conjunction or relative pronoun.

Property taxes rose sharply. ~~Although city~~ services declined.

written above "city": City

The battery is dead. ~~Which~~ means the car won't start.

written above "Which": This

(In the sentence above, the relative pronoun is replaced by *this,*
a word that can serve as the sentence's subject.)

Note, however, that deleting the subordinating conjunction
or relative pronoun is usually the least desirable way to revise a
sentence fragment, as it is likely to create two choppy sentences
and obscure the connection between them.

CLOSE-UP USING SENTENCE FRAGMENTS

Sentence fragments are often used in speech and informal writing as well as in journalism, advertising, and cre-
ative writing. In most college writing situations, however,
sentence fragments are not acceptable. Do not use them
without carefully considering their suitability for your audience and purpose.

CHAPTER 5

UNDERSTANDING AGREEMENT

Agreement is the correspondence between words in number, gender, and person. Subjects and verbs agree in **number** (singular or plural) and **person** (first, second, or third); pronouns and their antecedents agree in number, person, and **gender**.

See 11a4

5a Subject-Verb Agreement

See 6b1

Singular subjects have singular verbs, and plural subjects have plural verbs. **Present tense** verbs, except *be* and *have,* add *-s* or *-es* when the subject is third-person singular. Third-person singular subjects include nouns; the personal pronouns *he, she, it,* and *one;* and many indefinite pronouns.

The <u>President</u> <u>has</u> the power to veto congressional legislation.

<u>She</u> frequently <u>cites</u> statistics to support her points.

In every group <u>somebody</u> <u>emerges</u> as a natural leader.

Present tense verbs do not add *-s* or *-es* when the subject is a plural noun, a first-person or second-person pronoun (*I, we, you*), or a third-person plural pronoun (*they*).

<u>Experts</u> <u>recommend</u> that dieters avoid processed meat.

At this stratum, <u>we</u> <u>see</u> rocks dating back ten million years.

<u>They</u> <u>say</u> that some wealthy people default on their student loans.

In some special situations, subject-verb agreement can be troublesome.

(1) Words That Come between Subject and Verb

If a modifying phrase comes between subject and verb, the verb should agree with the subject, not with a word in the intervening phrase.

The <u>sound</u> of the drumbeats <u>builds</u> in intensity in *The Emperor Jones.*

The <u>games</u> won by the intramural team <u>are</u> few and far between.

This rule also applies to phrases introduced by *along with, as well as, in addition to, including,* and *together with.*

Heavy <u>rain</u>, along with high winds, <u>causes</u> hazardous driving conditions.

(2) Compound Subjects Joined by *and*

Compound subjects joined by *and* usually take plural verbs.

<u>Air bags and antilock brakes</u> <u>are</u> standard on all new models.

However, compound subjects joined by *and* that stand for a single idea or person are treated as a unit and used with singular verbs: <u>Rhythm and blues</u> <u>is</u> a forerunner of rock and roll.

In addition, when *each* or *every* precedes a compound subject joined by *and*, the subject takes a singular verb: <u>Every desk and file cabinet</u> <u>was</u> searched before the letter was found.

(3)   Compound Subjects Joined by *or*

Compound subjects joined by *or* or by *either . . . or* or *neither . . . nor* may take singular or plural verbs. The verb agrees with the closest noun.

<u>Either radiation treatments or chemotherapy</u> <u>is</u> combined with surgery for effective results.

<u>Either chemotherapy or radiation treatments</u> <u>are</u> combined with surgery for effective results.

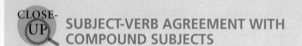

CLOSE-UP   SUBJECT-VERB AGREEMENT WITH COMPOUND SUBJECTS

When a compound subject is made up of one singular and one plural element, the verb agrees with the element nearest to it.

<u>Neither John nor his running mates</u> <u>wish</u> to contest the election.

<u>Neither his running mates nor John</u> <u>wishes</u> to contest the election.

(4) Indefinite Pronouns

Some **indefinite pronouns**—*both, many, few, several, others*—are always plural and take plural verbs. Most others—*another, anyone, everyone, one, each, either, neither, anything, everything, something, nothing, nobody,* and *somebody*—are singular and take singular verbs.

<u>Anyone</u> <u>is</u> welcome to apply for the scholarship.

<u>Each</u> of the chapters <u>includes</u> a review exercise.

A few indefinite pronouns—*some, all, any, more, most,* and *none*—can be singular or plural, depending on the noun they refer to.

<u>Some</u> of this trouble <u>is</u> to be expected. (*Some* refers to *trouble.*)

<u>Some</u> of the spectators <u>are</u> restless. (*Some* refers to *spectators.*)

(5) Collective Nouns

A **collective noun** names a group of persons or things—for instance, *navy, union, association, band.* When it refers to the group as a unit, a collective noun takes a singular verb; when it refers to the individuals or items that make up the group, it takes a plural verb.

To many people the <u>royal family</u> <u>symbolizes</u> Great Britain. (The family, as a unit, is the symbol.)

The <u>family</u> all <u>eat</u> at different times. (Each member eats separately.)

When a phrase that names a fixed amount—*three-quarters, twenty dollars, the majority*—is considered as a unit, it takes a singular verb; when it denotes parts of the whole, it takes a plural verb.

<u>Three-quarters</u> of his usual salary <u>is</u> not enough.

<u>Three-quarters</u> of the patients <u>improve</u> dramatically.

(6) Singular Subjects with Plural Forms

A singular subject takes a singular verb, even if its form is plural.

<u>Statistics</u> <u>deals</u> with the collection and analysis of data.

When such a word has a plural meaning, however, use a plural verb.

The <u>statistics</u> <u>prove</u> him wrong.

(7) Inverted Subject-Verb Order

Even when the verb comes before the subject, (as it does in questions and in sentences beginning with *there is* or *there are*), the subject and verb must agree.

<u>Is</u> <u>either</u> answer correct?

There <u>are</u> currently twelve <u>courts</u> of appeals in the federal system.

(8) Linking Verbs

A **linking verb** should agree with its subject, not with the subject complement.

See 8a

The <u>problem</u> <u>was</u> termites.

<u>Termites</u> <u>were</u> the problem.

(9) Relative Pronouns

When you use a **relative pronoun** (*who, which, that,* and so on) to introduce a dependent clause, the verb in that clause agrees with the pronoun's **antecedent,** the word to which the pronoun refers.

See B1.2

The farmer is among the <u>ones</u> who <u>suffer</u> during a grain embargo.

The farmer is the only <u>one</u> who <u>suffers</u> during a grain embargo.

5b Pronoun-Antecedent Agreement

Singular pronouns—such as *he, him, she, her, it, me, myself,* and *oneself*—should refer to singular antecedents. Plural pronouns—such as *we, us, they, them,* and *their*—should refer to plural antecedents.

(1) Compound Antecedents

In most cases, use a plural pronoun to refer to two or more antecedents connected by *and.*

<u>Mormonism and Christian Science</u> were similar in <u>their</u> beginnings.

Use a singular pronoun when a compound antecedent is preceded by *each* or *every.*

<u>Every programming language and software package</u> has <u>its</u> limitations.

Use a singular pronoun to refer to two or more singular antecedents linked by *or* or *nor.*

<u>Neither Thoreau nor Whitman</u> lived to see <u>his</u> work read widely.

When one part of a compound antecedent is singular and one part is plural, the pronoun agrees with the closer antecedent.

27

Neither the boy nor his parents had their seatbelts fastened.

(2) Collective Noun Antecedents

If the meaning of a collective noun antecedent is singular (as it will be in most cases), use a singular pronoun. If the meaning is plural, use a plural pronoun.

The teachers' union announced its plan to strike. (The members act as one.)

The team moved to their positions. (Each member acts individually.)

(3) Indefinite Pronoun Antecedents

See B1.2

Most **indefinite pronouns**—*each, either, neither, one, anyone,* and the like—are singular and are used with singular pronouns.

Neither of the men had his proposal ready by the deadline.

Each of these neighborhoods has its own traditions and values.

CLOSE-UP **PRONOUN-ANTECEDENT AGREEMENT**

In speech and popular writing, many people use the plural pronouns *they* or *their* with singular indefinite pronouns that refer to people, such as *someone, everyone,* and *nobody.*

Everyone can present their own viewpoint.

In college writing, however, never use a plural pronoun with a singular subject. Instead, you can use both the masculine and the feminine pronoun.

Everyone can present his or her own viewpoint.

Or you can make the sentence's subject plural.

All participants can present their own viewpoint.

The use of *his* alone to refer to a singular indefinite pronoun (Everyone can present *his* own viewpoint) is considered **sexist language**.

See 14d2

CHAPTER 6

USING VERBS CORRECTLY

6a Irregular Verbs

A **regular verb** forms both its past tense and its past participle by adding *-d* or *-ed*.

PRINCIPAL PARTS OF REGULAR VERBS

Base Form	*Past Tense Form*	*Past Participle*
smile	smiled	smiled
talk	talked	talked

Irregular verbs do not follow this pattern. The chart on pages 29–31 lists the principal parts of the most frequently used irregular verbs.

FREQUENTLY USED IRREGULAR VERBS

Base Form	*Past Tense Form*	*Past Participle*
arise	arose	arisen
awake	awoke, awaked	awoke, awaked
be	was/were	been
beat	beat	beaten
begin	began	begun
bend	bent	bent
bet	bet, betted	bet
bite	bit	bitten
blow	blew	blown
break	broke	broken
bring	brought	brought
build	built	built
burst	burst	burst
buy	bought	bought
catch	caught	caught
choose	chose	chosen
cling	clung	clung

continued on the following page

---

continued from the previous page

Base Form	Past Tense Form	Past Participle
come	came	come
cost	cost	cost
deal	dealt	dealt
dig	dug	dug
dive	dived, dove	dived
do	did	done
drag	dragged	dragged
draw	drew	drawn
drink	drank	drunk
drive	drove	driven
eat	ate	eaten
fall	fell	fallen
fight	fought	fought
find	found	found
fly	flew	flown
forget	forgot	forgotten, forgot
freeze	froze	frozen
get	got	gotten
give	gave	given
go	went	gone
grow	grew	grown
hang (suspend)	hung	hung
have	had	had
hear	heard	heard
keep	kept	kept
know	knew	known
lay	laid	laid
lead	led	led
lend	lent	lent
let	let	let
lie (recline)	lay	lain
make	made	made
prove	proved	proved, proven
read	read	read
ride	rode	ridden
ring	rang	rung
rise	rose	risen
run	ran	run
say	said	said
see	saw	seen
set (place)	set	set
shake	shook	shaken

continued on the following page

continued from the previous page

Base Form	Past Tense Form	Past Participle
shrink	shrank, shrunk	shrunk, shrunken
sing	sang	sung
sink	sank	sunk
sit	sat	sat
speak	spoke	spoken
speed	sped, speeded	sped, speeded
spin	spun	spun
spring	sprang	sprung
stand	stood	stood
steal	stole	stolen
strike	struck	struck, stricken
swear	swore	sworn
swim	swam	swum
swing	swung	swung
take	took	taken
teach	taught	taught
throw	threw	thrown
wake	woke, waked	waked, woken
wear	wore	worn
wring	wrung	wrung
write	wrote	written

CLOSE-UP IRREGULAR VERBS: *LIE/LAY* AND *SIT/SET*

Lie means "recline" and does not take an object ("He likes to *lie* on the floor"); *lay* means "place" or "put" and does take an object ("He wants to *lay* a rug on the floor"):

Base Form	Past Tense Form	Past Participle
lie	lay	lain
lay	laid	laid

Sit means "assume a seated position" and does not take an object ("She wants to *sit* on the table"); set means "place" or "put" and usually takes an object ("She wants to *set* a vase on the table"):

Base Form	Past Tense Form	Past Participle
sit	sat	sat
set	set	set

6b Tense

Tense is the form that a verb takes to indicate when an action occurred or when a condition existed.

ENGLISH VERB TENSES

Simple Tenses
Present (I *finish*, he or she *finishes*)
Past (I *finished*)
Future (I *will finish*)

Perfect Tenses
Present perfect (I *have finished*, he or she *has finished*)
Past perfect (I *had finished*)
Future perfect (I *will have finished*)

Progressive Tenses
Present progressive (I *am finishing*, he or she *is finishing*)
Past progressive (I *was finishing*)
Future progressive (I *will be finishing*)
Present perfect progressive (I *have been finishing*)
Past perfect progressive (I *had been finishing*)
Future perfect progressive (I *will have been finishing*)

---

(1) Using the Simple Tenses

The **simple tenses** include *present*, *past*, and *future*.

The **present tense** usually indicates an action taking place at the time it is expressed in speech or writing or an action that occurs regularly.

I <u>see</u> your point. (an action taking place when it is expressed)

He <u>wears</u> wool in the winter. (an action that occurs regularly)

CLOSE-UP SPECIAL USES OF THE PRESENT TENSE

The present tense has four special uses.

To Indicate Future Time: The grades <u>arrive</u> next Thursday.

To State a Generally Held Belief: Studying <u>pays</u> off.

continued on the following page

continued from the previous page

TO STATE A SCIENTIFIC TRUTH: An object at rest <u>tends</u> to stay at rest.

TO DISCUSS A LITERARY WORK: *Family Installments* <u>tells</u> the story of a Puerto Rican family.

The **past tense** indicates that an action has already taken place.

John Glenn <u>orbited</u> the Earth three times on February 20, 1962. (an action completed in the past)

As a young man, Mark Twin <u>traveled</u> through the Southwest. (an action that recurred in the past but did not extend into the present)

The **future tense** indicates that an action will or is likely to take place.

Halley's Comet <u>will reappear</u> in 2061. (a future action that will definitely occur)

The land boom in Nevada <u>will</u> probably <u>continue</u>. (a future action that is likely to occur)

(2) Using the Perfect Tenses

The **perfect tenses** designate actions that were or will be completed before other actions or conditions. The perfect tenses are formed with the appropriate tense form of the auxiliary verb *have* plus the past participle.

The **present perfect** tense can indicate two types of continuing action beginning in the past.

Dr. Kim <u>has finished</u> studying the effects of BHA on rats. (an action that began in the past and is finished at the present time)

My mother <u>has invested</u> her money wisely. (an action that began in the past and extends into the present)

The **past perfect** tense indicates an action occurring before a certain time in the past.

By 1946 engineers <u>had built</u> the first electronic digital computer.

The **future perfect** tense indicates that an action will be finished by a certain future time.

By Tuesday the transit authority <u>will have run</u> out of money.

(3) Using the Progressive Tenses

The **progressive tenses** express continuing action. They are formed with the appropriate tense of the verb *be* plus the present participle.

The **present progressive** tense indicates that something is happening at the time it is expressed in speech or writing.

> The volcano is erupting, and lava is flowing toward the town.

The **past progressive** tense indicates two kinds of past action.

> Roderick Usher's actions were becoming increasingly bizarre. (a continuing action in the past)

> The French revolutionary Marat was stabbed to death while he was bathing. (an action occurring at the same time in the past as another action)

The **future progressive** tense indicates a continuing action in the future.

> The treasury secretary will be carefully monitoring the money supply.

The **present perfect progressive** tense indicates action continuing from the past into the present and possibly into the future.

> Rescuers have been working around the clock.

The **past perfect progressive** tense indicates that a past action went on until another one occurred.

> Before President Kennedy was assassinated, he had been working on civil rights legislation.

The **future perfect progressive** tense indicates that an action will continue until a certain future time.

> By eleven o'clock we will have been driving for seven hours.

6c Mood

Mood is the form a verb takes to indicate whether a writer is making a statement, asking a question, giving a command, or expressing a wish or a contrary-to-fact statement. There are three moods in English: the *indicative,* the *imperative,* and the *subjunctive.*

The **indicative** mood states a fact, expresses an opinion, or asks a question: Jackie Robinson had an impact on professional baseball.

The **imperative** mood is used in commands and direct requests: <u>Use</u> a dictionary.

The **subjunctive** mood causes the greatest difficulty for writers. The **present subjunctive** uses the base form of the verb, regardless of the subject. The **past subjunctive** has the same form as the past tense of the verb. (The auxiliary verb *be*, however, takes the form *were* regardless of the number or person of the subject.)

The present subjunctive is used in *that* clauses after words such as *ask, suggest, require, recommend,* and *demand.*

The report recommended that doctors <u>be</u> more flexible.

Captain Ahab insisted that his crew <u>hunt</u> the white whale.

The past subjunctive is used in **conditional statements** (statements beginning with *if* or *as if* that are contrary to fact and statements that express a wish).

If John <u>were</u> here, he could see Marsha. (John is not here.)

The father acted as if he <u>were</u> having the baby. (The father couldn't be having the baby.)

I wish I <u>were</u> more organized. (expresses a wish)

6d Voice

Voice is the form a verb takes to indicate whether its subject acts or is acted upon. When the subject of a verb does something—that is, acts—the verb is in the **active voice.** When the subject of a verb receives the action—that is, is acted upon—the verb is in the **passive voice.**

ACTIVE VOICE: Hart Crane <u>wrote</u> *The Bridge.*

PASSIVE VOICE: *The Bridge* <u>was written</u> by Hart Crane.

Because the active voice emphasizes the doer of an action, it is usually clearer and more emphatic than the passive voice. Whenever possible, use active voice in your college writing.

CHAPTER 7

USING PRONOUNS CORRECTLY

7a Understanding Pronoun Case

Pronouns change **case** to indicate their function in a sentence. English has three cases: *subjective, objective,* and *possessive.*

PRONOUN CASE FORMS

Subjective

| I | he,
she | it | we | you | they | who | whoever |

Objective

| me | him,
her | it | us | you | them | whom | whomever |

Possessive

| my | his,
her | its | our | your | their | whose | |
| (mine) | (hers) | | (ours) | (yours) | (theirs) | | |

---

(1) Subjective Case

A pronoun takes the **subjective case** in the following situations.

SUBJECT OF A VERB: <u>I</u> bought a new mountain bike.

SUBJECT COMPLEMENT: It was <u>he</u> for whom the men were looking.

APPOSITIVE IDENTIFYING SUBJECT: Both scientists, <u>Oppenheimer and he</u>, worked on the atomic bomb.

(2) Objective Case

A pronoun takes the **objective case** in these situations.

DIRECT OBJECT: Our sociology teacher likes Adam and <u>me</u>.

INDIRECT OBJECT: The plumber's bill gave <u>him</u> quite a shock.

OBJECT OF A PREPOSITION: Between <u>us</u> we own ten shares of stock.

APPOSITIVE IDENTIFYING AN OBJECT: Rachel discussed both authors, <u>Hannah Arendt and her</u>.

CLOSE-UP

PRONOUN CASE IN COMPOUND CONSTRUCTIONS

I is not necessarily more appropriate than *me*. In compound constructions like the following, *me* is correct.

Just between you and <u>me</u> [not *I*], I think we're going to have a quiz. (*Me* is the object of the preposition *between*.)

(3) Possessive Case

A pronoun takes the **possessive case** when it indicates ownership (*our* car, *your* book). Remember to use the possessive, not the objective, case before a <u>gerund</u>.

See
B1.3

Napoleon approved of <u>their</u> [not *them*] ruling Naples. (*Ruling* is a gerund.)

Determining Pronoun Case in Special Situations

(1) Implied Comparisons with *Than* or *As*

When a sentence containing an implied comparison ends with a pronoun, your meaning dictates your choice of pronoun.

Darcy likes John more than <u>I</u>. (more than I like John)

Darcy likes John more than <u>me</u>. (more than she likes me)

(2) *Who* and *Whom*

The case of the pronouns *who* and *whom* depends on their function *within their own clause*. When a pronoun serves as the subject of its clause, use *who* or *whoever;* when it functions as an object, use *whom* or *whomever*.

The Salvation Army gives food and shelter to <u>whoever</u> is in need. (*Whoever* is the subject of a dependent clause.)

I wonder <u>whom</u> jazz musician Miles Davis influenced. (*Whom* is the object of *influenced* in the dependent clause.)

CLOSE-UP

PRONOUN CASE IN QUESTIONS

To determine the case of *who* at the beginning of a question, use a personal pronoun to answer the question.

continued on the following page

continued from the previous page

The case of *who* should be the same as the case of the personal pronoun.

> <u>Who</u> wrote *The Age of Innocence?* <u>She</u> wrote it. (subject)
>
> <u>Whom</u> do you support for mayor? I support <u>her</u>. (object)

(3) Appositives

An **appositive** is a noun or noun phrase that identifies or renames a word that precedes it. The case of a pronoun in an appositive depends on the function of the word that it describes.

> We heard two Motown recording artists, Smokey Robinson and <u>him</u>. (*Recording artists* is the object of the verb *heard,* so the pronoun in the appositive *Smokey Robinson and him* takes the objective case.)

> Two Motown recording artists, Smokey Robinson and <u>he</u>, recorded for Motown Records. (*Recording artists* is the subject of the sentence, so the pronoun in the appositive *Smokey Robinson and he* takes the subjective case.)

(4) *We* and *Us* before a Noun

When a first-person plural pronoun precedes a noun, the case of the pronoun depends on the way the noun functions in the sentence.

> <u>We</u> women must stick together. (*Women* is the subject of the sentence, so the pronoun *we* must be in the subjective case.)

> Teachers make learning easy for <u>us</u> students. (*Students* is the object of the preposition *for,* so the pronoun *us* must be in the objective case.)

7c Revising Common Errors of Pronoun Reference

An **antecedent** is the word or word group to which a pronoun refers. The connection between a pronoun and its antecedent should always be clear.

(1) Ambiguous Antecedents

Sometimes a pronoun—for example, *this, that, which,* or *it*—appears to refer to more than one antecedent. In such cases, substitute a noun for the pronoun.

The accountant took out his calculator and completed the
tax return. Then, he put ~~it~~ *the calculator* into his briefcase.

Sometimes a pronoun does not seem to refer to any specific antecedent. In such cases, supply a noun to clarify the reference.

Some one-celled organisms contain chlorophyll yet are considered animals. This *paradox* illustrates the difficulty of classifying
single-celled organisms.

(2) Remote Antecedents
The farther a pronoun is from its antecedent, the more difficult it is for readers to make a connection between them.

During the mid-1800s, many Czechs began to immigrate to
America. By 1860, about 23,000 Czechs had left their country. By 1900, 13,000 Czech immigrants were coming to *America's* ~~its~~
shores each year.

(3) Nonexistent Antecedents
Sometimes a pronoun refers to a nonexistent antecedent.

Our township has decided to build a computer lab in the elementary school. *Teachers* ~~They~~ feel that fourth-graders should begin
using computers.

(4) *Who, Which,* and *That*
In general, *who* refers to people or to animals that have
names. *Which* and *that* refer to objects, events, or unnamed animals and sometimes to groups of people.

David Henry Hwang, <u>who</u> wrote the Tony Award-winning
play *M. Butterfly,* also wrote *Family Devotions* and *FOB.*

The spotted owl, <u>which</u> lives in old growth forests, is in danger of extinction.

Houses <u>that</u> are built today are usually more energy efficient
than those built twenty years ago.

PART 3

WRITING EFFECTIVE SENTENCES

CHAPTER 8

USING ADJECTIVES AND ADVERBS CORRECTLY

Adjectives modify nouns and pronouns. **Adverbs** modify verbs; adjectives; other adverbs; or entire phrases, clauses, or sentences.

The *function* of a word, not its *form*, determines whether it is classified as an adjective or as an adverb. Many adverbs (such as *immediately* and *hopelessly*) end in *-ly*, but others (such as *almost* and *very*) do not. Moreover, some words that end in *-ly* (such as *lively*) are adjectives.

8a Using Adjectives as Subject Complements

Be sure to use an adjective, not an adverb, as a subject complement. A **subject complement** is a word that follows a linking verb and modifies the sentence's subject, not its verb. (A **linking verb** does not show physical or emotional action. *Seem, appear, believe, become, grow, turn, remain, prove, look, sound, smell, taste, feel,* and the forms of the verb *be* are or can be used as linking verbs.)

See
B1.3

> Michelle seemed <u>brave</u>. (*Seemed* shows no action and is therefore a linking verb. Because *brave* is a subject complement that modifies the noun *Michelle*, it takes the adjective form.)

> Michelle smiled <u>bravely</u>. (*Smiled* shows action, so it is not a linking verb. *Bravely* modifies *smiled*, so it takes the adverb form.)

Sometimes the same verb can function as either a linking verb or an action verb. Compare these two sentences.

> He looked <u>hungry</u>. (*Hungry* modifies the subject.)

> He looked <u>hungrily</u> at the sandwich. (*Hungrily* modifies the verb.)

8b Using Adverbs Appropriately

Be sure to use an adverb, not an adjective, to modify verbs; adjectives; other adverbs; or entire phrases, clauses, or sentences.

Most students did ~~great~~ *very well* on the midterm.

My parents dress a lot more conservative *ly* than my friends do.

CLOSE-UP USING ADJECTIVES AND ADVERBS

In informal speech, adjective forms such as *good, bad, sure, real, slow, quick,* and *loud* are often used to modify verbs, adjectives, and adverbs. Avoid these informal modifiers in college writing.

The program ran ~~real good~~ *really well* the first time we tried it, but the new system performed ~~bad~~ *badly*.

8c Using Comparative and Superlative Forms

COMPARATIVE AND SUPERLATIVE FORMS

Form	Function	Example
Positive	Describes a quality; indicates no comparisons	big
Comparative	Indicates comparisons between *two* qualities (greater or lesser)	bigger
Superlative	Indicates comparisons among *more than two* qualities (greatest or least)	biggest

NOTE: Some adverbs, particularly those indicating time, place, and degree (*almost, very, here, yesterday,* and *immediately*), do not have comparative or superlative forms.

(1) Regular Comparatives and Superlatives

Never use the superlative when comparing only two things.

Stacy is the ~~oldest~~ *older* of the two sisters.

Never use the comparative when comparing more than two things.

We chose the ~~earlier~~ ^{earliest} of the four appointments.

To form the comparative and superlative, all one-syllable adjectives and many two-syllable adjectives (particularly those that end in *-y, -ly, -le, -er,* and *-ow*) add *-er* or *-est:* slow<u>er</u>, funni<u>er</u>; slow<u>est</u>, funni<u>est</u>. (Note that a final *y* becomes *i* before the *-er* or *-est* is added.)

Other two-syllable adjectives and all long adjectives form the comparative with *more* and the superlative with *most:* <u>more</u> famous, <u>more</u> incredible; <u>most</u> famous, <u>most</u> incredible.

Adverbs ending in *-ly* also form the comparative with *more* and the superlative with *most:* <u>more</u> slowly; <u>most</u> slowly. Other adverbs use the *-er* and *-est* endings: soon<u>er</u>; soon<u>est</u>.

All adjectives and adverbs indicate a lesser degree with *less* (<u>less</u> lovely; <u>less</u> slowly) and the least degree with *least* (<u>least</u> lovely; <u>least</u> slowly).

CLOSE-UP   USING COMPARATIVES AND SUPERLATIVES

Never use both *more* and *-er* to form the comparative or both *most* and *-est* to form the superlative.

Nothing could have been ~~more~~ easier.

Jack is the ~~most~~ meanest person in town.

---

(2) Irregular Comparatives and Superlatives

Some adjectives and adverbs have irregular comparative and superlative forms. Instead of adding a word or an ending to the positive form, they use different words to indicate the comparative and the superlative.

IRREGULAR COMPARATIVES AND SUPERLATIVES

	Positive	*Comparative*	*Superlative*
Adjectives:	good	better	best
	bad	worse	worst
	a little	less	least
	many, some, much	more	most
Adverbs:	well	better	best
	badly	worse	worst

45

NOTE: Many adjectives and adverbs can logically exist only in the positive degree. For example, words like *perfect, unique, excellent, impossible,* and *dead* cannot have comparative or superlative forms.

I read ~~the most~~ *an* excellent story.

The vase in her collection was ~~very~~ unique.

CHAPTER 9

WRITING VARIED SENTENCES

9a Using Compound and Complex Sentences

Paragraphs that mix simple, compound, and complex sentences are generally more interesting and easier to follow than those that do not.

(1) Compound Sentences

A **compound sentence** is created when two or more independent clauses are joined with *coordinating conjunctions, transitional words and phrases, correlative conjunctions, semicolons,* or *colons.*

Coordinating Conjunction
The pianist made several mistakes, <u>but</u> the concert was still a success.

NOTE: Use a comma before a coordinating conjunction—*and, or, nor, but, for, so,* and *yet*—that joins two <u>**independent clauses**</u>.

See 16a

Transitional Words and Phrases
The saxophone does not belong to the brass family; <u>in fact</u>, it is a member of the woodwind family.

NOTE: Use a semicolon—not a comma—before a transitional word or phrase that joins two independent clauses. Frequently used <u>**transitional words and phrases**</u> include conjunctive adverbs like *consequently, finally, still,* and *thus* as well as expressions like *for example, in fact, on the other hand,* and *for instance.*

See 2b

Correlative Conjunctions
<u>Either</u> he left his coat in his locker, <u>or</u> he left it on the bus.
Semicolons
Alaska is the largest state; Rhode Island is the smallest.
Colons
He got his orders: he was to leave for France on Sunday.

(2) Complex Sentences

A **complex sentence** consists of one independent clause and at least one dependent clause. A **subordinating conjunction** or **relative pronoun** links the independent and dependent clauses and indicates the relationship between them.

(dependent clause)   (independent clause)
[After the town was evacuated], [the hurricane began].

(independent clause)   (dependent clause)
[Officials watched the storm], [which threatened to destroy the town].

(dependent clause)
Town officials, [who were very concerned], watched the storm.

FREQUENTLY USED SUBORDINATING CONJUNCTIONS

after	before	until
although	if	when
as	once	whenever
as if	since	where
as though	that	wherever
because	unless	while

RELATIVE PRONOUNS

that	whatever	who (whose, whom)
what	which	whoever (whomever)

9b Varying Sentence Length

Strings of short simple sentences can be tedious—and sometimes hard to follow, as the following paragraph indicates.

> John Peter Zenger was a newspaper editor. He waged and won an important battle for freedom of the press in America. He criticized the policies of the British governor. He was charged with criminal libel as a result. Zenger's lawyers were disbarred by the governor. Andrew Hamilton defended him. Hamilton convinced the jury that Zenger's criticisms were true. Therefore, the statements were not libelous.

You can revise such sentences by using *coordination, subordination,* or *embedding* to combine them with adjacent sentences.

Coordination pairs similar elements—words, phrases, or clauses—giving equal weight to each.

Two choppy sentences linked with *and,* creating compound sentence

> John Peter Zenger was a newspaper editor. He waged and won an important battle for freedom of the press in America. <u>He criticized the policies of the British governor, and as a result, he was charged with criminal libel</u>. Zenger's lawyers were disbarred by the governor. Andrew Hamilton defended him. Hamilton convinced the jury that Zenger's criticisms were true. Therefore, the statements were not libelous.

Subordination places the more important idea in an independent clause and the less important idea in a dependent clause.

John Peter Zenger was a newspaper editor who waged and won an important battle for freedom of the press in America. He criticized the policies of the British governor, and as a result, he was charged with criminal libel. When Zenger's lawyers were disbarred by the governor, Andrew Hamilton defended him. Hamilton convinced the jury that Zenger's criticisms were true. Therefore, the statements were not libelous.

Simple sentences become dependent clauses, creating complex sentences

Embedding is the working of additional words and phrases into sentences.

John Peter Zenger was a newspaper editor who waged and won an important battle for freedom of the press in America. He criticized the policies of the British governor, and as a result, he was charged with criminal libel. When Zenger's lawyers were disbarred by the governor, Andrew Hamilton defended him, convincing the jury that Zenger's criticisms were true. Therefore, the statements were not libelous.

The sentence Hamilton convinced the jury… becomes the phrase convincing the jury

This final revision uses coordination, subordination, and embedding to vary sentence length but retains the final short simple sentence for emphasis.

9c Varying Sentence Types

To achieve sentence variety, mix __declarative__ sentences (statements) with occasional __imperative__ sentences (commands or requests), __exclamatory__ sentences, and **rhetorical questions** (questions that the reader is not expected to answer).

See B2.2

Local television newscasts seem to be delivering less and less news. Although we tune in to be updated on local, national, and world events, only about 30 percent of most newscasts is devoted to news. The remaining time is spent on feature stories, advertising, weather, sports, and casual conversation between anchors. Given this focus on "soft" material, what options do those of us wishing to find out what happened in the world have? [**rhetorical question**] Critics of local television have a few suggestions. First, write to your local station's management voicing your concern; then, try to get others to sign a petition. [**imperatives**] If changes are not made, you can turn off your television and read the newspaper! [**exclamation**]

9d Varying Sentence Openings

Rather than begin every sentence with the subject, begin with modifying words, phrases, or clauses.

Words
<u>Proud</u> and <u>relieved</u>, they watched their daughter receive her diploma. (adjectives)

Phrases
<u>For better or worse</u>, credit cards are now widely available to college students. (prepositional phrase)

<u>Located on the west coast of Great Britain</u>, Wales is part of the United Kingdom. (participial phrase)

<u>His interests widening</u>, Picasso designed ballet sets and illustrated books. (absolute phrase)

Clauses
<u>After Woodrow Wilson was incapacitated by a stroke</u>, his wife unofficially performed many presidential duties. (adverb clause)

9e Varying Standard Word Order

(1) Inverting Word Order

You can vary standard subject-verb-object (or complement) word order by placing the complement or direct object *before* the verb instead of in its conventional position or by placing the verb *before* the subject instead of after it.

    (object) (verb)
A cheery smile he had for everyone.
       (subject)

  (complement)
Especially useful was the book's index.
          (verb)   (subject)

These strategies are useful because they draw attention to the word or word group that appears in an unexpected place—but inverted word order can be distracting, so use it in moderation.

(2) Separating Subject from Verb

You can place words or phrases between the subject and verb—but be sure that the word group does not obscure the connection between subject and verb or create an **agreement** error.

See
5a1

   (subject)   (verb)
Many <u>states</u>, hoping to reduce needless fatalities, <u>require</u> that children ride in government-approved child safety seats.

CHAPTER 10

WRITING CONCISE SENTENCES

A sentence is not concise simply because it is short; a concise sentence contains only the words necessary to make its point.

10a Eliminating Nonessential Words

Whenever possible, delete nonessential words—*deadwood, utility words,* and *circumlocution*—from your writing.

(1) Deleting Deadwood

Deadwood refers to unnecessary phrases that take up space and add nothing to meaning.

~~There were~~ Many factors ~~that~~ influenced his decision to become a priest.

Shoppers ~~who are~~ looking for bargains often go to outlets.

They played a̲ an exhausting racquetball game ~~that was exhausting~~.

~~In this~~ This article ~~it~~ discusses lead poisoning.

Deadwood also includes unnecessary statements of opinion, such as *I feel, it seems to me,* and *in my opinion.*

~~In my opinion, the~~ The characters seem undeveloped.

~~As far as I'm concerned, this~~ This course looks interesting.

(2) Deleting or Replacing Utility Words

Utility words are simply fillers; they contribute nothing to a sentence. Utility words include nouns with imprecise meanings (*factor, situation, type, aspect,* and so on); adjectives so general that they are almost meaningless (*good, bad, important*); and common adverbs denoting degree (*basically, very, definitely*).

~~The registration situation~~ Registration was disorganized.

The scholarship offered Fran a̲ an ~~good~~ opportunity to study Spanish.

Writing Concise Sentences

It was ~~actually~~ a worthwhile book, but I didn't ~~completely~~ finish it.

(3) Avoiding Circumlocution

Taking a roundabout way to say something (using ten words when five will do) is called **circumlocution.** Instead of complicated phrases and constructions, use short, concrete, specific words and phrases and come right to the point.

The

probably

~~It is not unlikely that the~~ trend toward smaller cars will ‸continue.

while

Joel was in the army ~~during the same time that~~ I was in college.

 REVISING WORDY PHRASES

If you cannot edit a wordy construction, substitute a more concise, more direct term.

Wordy	*Concise*
at the present time	now
due to the fact that	because
in the vicinity of	near
have the ability to	be able to

 Eliminating Unnecessary Repetition

Unnecessary repetition and redundant word groups can annoy readers and obscure your meaning. Correct unnecessary repetition by using one of the following strategies.

(1) Deleting Repeated Words

The childhood disease chicken pox occasionally leads to dangerous complications, such as ~~the disease known as~~ Reye's syndrome.

(2) Substituting a Pronoun

Agatha Christie's Miss Marple has solved many crimes. *The*
her
Murder at the Vicarage was one of ~~Miss Marple's~~ most challenging cases.

(3) Creating Appositives

Red Barber, ~~was~~ a sportscaster, ~~He~~ was known for his colorful expressions.

(4) Creating Compounds

In 1964, Ted Briggs was discharged from the Air Force, ~~He~~
and
~~then~~ got a job with Maxwell Data Processing, ~~He~~ married
Susan Thompson ~~that same year~~.

(5) Creating Complex Sentences

which
Americans value freedom of speech, ~~Freedom of speech~~ is
guaranteed by the First Amendment.

10c Tightening Rambling Sentences

The combination of nonessential words, unnecessary repetition, and complicated syntax creates **rambling sentences.** Revising rambling sentences frequently requires extensive editing.

(1) Eliminating Excessive Coordination

When you string a series of clauses together with coordinating conjunctions, you create a rambling, unfocused **compound sentence**. To revise such sentences, first identify the main idea or ideas and then subordinate the supporting details.

See 9a1

Benjamin Franklin, ~~was~~ the son of a candlemaker, ~~but he~~
an
later apprenticed with his half-brother as a printer, ~~and in~~
that
~~1730 this~~ experience led to his buying *The Pennsylvania*
which
Gazette, ~~and~~ he managed ~~this periodical~~ with great success.

(2) Eliminating Adjective Clauses

A series of **adjective clauses** is also likely to produce a rambling sentence. To revise, substitute concise modifying words or phrases for the adjective clauses.

See B2.3

Moby-Dick, ~~which is~~ a novel about a white whale, was writ-
revised the first draft at the urging of his
ten by Herman Melville, who ~~was friendly with~~ Nathaniel
Hawthorne, ~~who encouraged him to revise the first draft~~.

(3) Eliminating Unnecessary Passive Constructions

See 6d

Excessive use of the **passive voice** can make sentences ramble. Correct this problem by changing passive to active voice.

> $\overset{\text{Concerned Americans are organizing}}{\wedge}$ "Buy American" rallies, ~~are being organized by concerned~~ $\overset{\text{hoping}}{\text{Americans who hope}}$ that ~~jobs can be saved by~~ such gatherings, can save jobs.

(4) Eliminating Wordy Prepositional Phrases

See B2.3

Substitute adjectives or adverbs for wordy **prepositional phrases**.

> $\overset{\text{dangerous}}{\text{The trip was}}$ ~~one of danger~~ but $\overset{\text{exciting}}{\text{~~also one of excitement~~}}$.

> $\overset{\text{confidently}}{\text{He spoke}}$ ~~in a confident manner~~ and $\overset{\text{authoritatively}}{\text{~~with a lot of authority~~}}$.

(5) Eliminating Wordy Noun Constructions

See B2.3

Substitute strong verbs for wordy **noun phrases**.

> $\overset{\text{decided}}{\text{We have}}$ ~~made the decision~~ to postpone the meeting until ~~the~~ ~~appearance of~~ all the board members $\overset{\text{appear}}{\wedge}$

CHAPTER 11

AVOIDING AWKWARD OR CONFUSING SENTENCES

The most common causes of confusing sentences are *unwarranted shifts, mixed constructions, faulty predication*, and *illogical comparisons*.

11a Shifts

(1) Shifts in Tense

See 6b

Verb <u>tense</u> in a sentence or in a related group of sentences should not shift without good reason—to indicate changes of time, for example.

The Wizard of Oz <u>is</u> a film that has enchanted audiences since it <u>was made</u> in 1939. (acceptable shift from present to past)

Unwarranted shifts can mislead readers and obscure your meaning.

I registered for the course because I thought it sounded interesting. However, after the first week I ~~start~~ started having trouble understanding the lectures.

On the Road is a novel about friends who ~~drove~~ drive across the United States in the 1950s.

(2) Shifts in Voice

See 6d

Unwarranted shifts from active to passive <u>voice</u> can be confusing. In the following sentence, for instance, the shift from active (*wrote*) to passive (*was written*) makes it unclear who wrote *The Great Gatsby*.

F. Scott Fitzgerald wrote *This Side of Paradise,* and later wrote *The Great Gatsby.* ~~was written.~~

CLOSE-UP   SHIFTS IN VOICE

Sometimes a shift from active to passive voice may be necessary to give a sentence proper emphasis.

Even though consumers <u>protested</u>, the sales tax <u>was increased</u>.

To say *the legislature increased the sales tax* would draw the emphasis of the sentence away from *consumers*.

(3) Shifts in Mood

See 6c

Unnecessary shifts in **mood** can also be confusing. The following sentence shifts from the imperative to the indicative mood.

Next, heat the mixture in a test tube, and ~~you should make~~ ^{be} sure it does not boil.

(4) Shifts in Person and Number

Person indicates who is speaking (first person—*I, we*), who is spoken to (second person—*you*), and who is spoken about (third person—*he, she, it,* and *they*). Unwarranted shifts between the second and the third person cause most errors.

When ~~someone~~ ^{you} looks for a car loan, you compare the interest rates of several banks.

Number indicates one (singular—*novel, it*) or more than one (plural—*novels, they, them*). Singular pronouns should refer to singular **antecedents** and plural pronouns to plural antecedents.

See 5b

If a person does not study regularly, ~~they~~ ^{he or she} will have a difficult time passing Spanish.

11b   Mixed Constructions

A **mixed construction** is created when a sentence begins with one grammatical strategy and then shifts to another. To avoid such errors, be sure you do not use a dependent clause, prepositional phrase, or independent clause as your sentence's subject.

Because she studies every day, ~~explains why~~ she gets good

grades. (dependent clause used as a subject)

By calling for information, you can ~~is the way to~~ learn more about the

benefits of ROTC. (prepositional phrase used as a subject)

Being ~~He was~~ late ~~was wh~~at made him miss Act 1. (independent

clause used as a subject)

11c Faulty Predication

Faulty predication occurs when a sentence's predicate does
not logically complete its subject. Faulty predication is especially common in sentences that contain a form of the verb *be*
and a subject complement.

Mounting costs and decreasing revenues caused ~~were~~ the downfall

of the hospital.

Faulty predication also occurs in sentences that contain a
construction like *is where, is when,* or *the reason is because. Is*
must be preceded and followed by nouns or noun phrases.

Taxidermy is the construction of ~~where you construct~~ a lifelike representation of

an animal from its preserved skin.

The reason we drive is that ~~because~~ we are afraid to fly.

CHAPTER 12

USING PARALLELISM

Parallelism is the use of matching words, phrases, clauses, or sentence structures to express equivalent ideas. Effective parallelism adds unity, balance, and force to your writing.

12a Using Parallelism Effectively

(1) With Items in a Series

<u>Eat</u>, <u>drink</u>, and <u>be</u> merry.

<u>Baby food consumption</u>, <u>toy production</u>, and <u>marijuana use</u> are likely to decline as the US population grows older.

(2) With Paired Items

The thank-you note was <u>short</u> but <u>sweet</u>.

The designer paid attention not only <u>to color</u> but also <u>to texture</u>.

Either <u>repeat physics</u> or <u>take calculus</u>.

Richard Wright and James Baldwin chose <u>to live in Paris</u> rather than <u>to remain in the United States</u>.

<u>Ask not what your country can do for you</u>; <u>ask what you can do for your country</u>. (John F. Kennedy, *inaugural address*)

Correlative conjunctions such as *not only/but also* and *either/or* often link paired elements, as does the word *than*.

See
A1.3:
27e1 **NOTE:** Elements in <u>lists</u> and <u>outlines</u> should also be parallel.

12b Revising Faulty Parallelism

Avoid **faulty parallelism** by making sure elements that have the same function in a sentence are not presented in parallel terms.

Many developing countries lack sufficient housing, sufficient food, and ~~their~~ ^{sufficient} health-care facilities.~~are also insufficient.~~

parallelism 12b

To create parallelism, match nouns with nouns, verbs with verbs, and phrases or clauses with similarly constructed phrases or clauses.

Popular exercises for men and women include aerobic dancing, weight ~~lifters~~ lifting, and jogging.

I look forward to hearing from you and to ~~have~~ having an opportunity to tell you more about myself.

Although the use of similar grammatical structures may sometimes be enough to convey parallelism, sentences are even clearer if other key words are also parallel. In the following sentence, repeating the preposition *by* makes it clear that *not* applies only to the first phrase.

Computerization has helped industry by not allowing labor costs to skyrocket, ∧by increasing the speed of production, and ∧by improving efficiency.

CHAPTER 13

PLACING MODIFIERS CAREFULLY

A modifier should be placed close to its **headword,** the word or phrase it modifies. **Faulty modification** is the confusing placement of modifiers or the modification of nonexistent words.

13a Revising Misplaced Modifiers

A **misplaced modifier** is a word or word group whose placement suggests that it modifies one word or phrase when it is intended to modify another.

(1) Placing Modifying Words Precisely

Limiting modifiers such as *almost, only, even,* and *just* should always immediately precede the words they modify. A different placement will change the meaning of a sentence.

Nick *just* set up camp at the edge of town. (He did it just now.)

Just Nick set up camp at the edge of town. (He did it alone.)

Nick set up camp *just* at the edge of town. (His camp was precisely at the edge.)

When a limiting modifier is placed so that it is not clear whether it modifies a word before it or one after it, it is called a *squinting modifier.*

The life that everyone thought would fulfill her <u>totally</u> bored her.

To correct a squinting modifier, place the modifier so that it clearly modifies its headword.

The life that everyone thought would <u>totally</u> fulfill her bored her. (She was expected to be totally fulfilled.)

The life that everyone thought would fulfill her bored her <u>totally</u>. (She was totally bored.)

(2) Repositioning Misplaced Phrases

Roller-skating along the shore,
∧ Jane watched the boats. ~~roller skating along the shore.~~

Created by a famous artist,
∧*Venus de Milo* is a statue ~~created by a famous artist~~ with no arms.

(3) Repositioning Misplaced Dependent Clauses

, which will benefit everyone,
This diet program∧will limit the consumption of possible carcinogens~~, which will benefit everyone~~.

After they had a glass of wine, the
~~The~~ parents checked to see that the children were sleeping. ~~after they had a glass of wine~~.

13b Revising Intrusive Modifiers

An **intrusive modifier** interrupts a sentence, making it difficult to understand.

Revise when a long modifying phrase comes between an auxiliary verb and a main verb.

Without
~~She~~ had~~, without~~ giving it a second thought or considering
she had
the consequences,∧planned to reenlist.

Revise when modifiers awkwardly interrupt an infinitive, coming between the word *to* and the base form of the verb.

defeat his opponent
He hoped to∧quickly and easily, ~~defeat his opponent~~.

13c Revising Dangling Modifiers

A **dangling modifier** is a word or phrase that cannot logically modify any word or word group in the sentence.

<u>Using this drug</u>, many undesirable side effects are experienced.

Using this drug appears to modify *side effects*, but this interpretation makes no sense. Because its true headword does not appear in the sentence, the modifier dangles. One way to correct the dangling modifier is to add a word or word group that it can logically modify.

Using this drug, <u>patients experience</u> many undesirable side effects.

Another way to correct the dangling modifier is to change it into a dependent clause.

61

Many undesirable side effects are experienced <u>when this drug is used</u>.

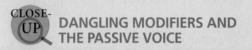

CLOSE-UP DANGLING MODIFIERS AND THE PASSIVE VOICE

See
6d

Most sentences that include dangling modifiers are in the passive voice and do not indicate a headword. Changing the **passive voice** to **active voice** corrects the dangling modifier by changing the subject of the sentence's main clause to a word that the dangling modifier can logically modify.

CHAPTER 14

CHOOSING THE RIGHT WORD

14a Avoiding Jargon

Jargon, the specialized or technical vocabulary of a trade, profession, or academic discipline, is useful for communicating in the field for which it was developed, but outside that field it is often imprecise or confusing.

JARGON: The patient had an acute myocardial infarction.

TRANSLATION: The patient had a heart attack.

In general, use vocabulary that is appropriate for your audience and purpose.

14b Avoiding Pretentious Diction

Good writing is clear writing, and pompous or flowery language is no substitute for clarity. Revise to eliminate **pretentious diction,** inappropriately elevated and wordy language.

As I fell ~~into slumber~~ asleep, I ~~cogitated~~ thought about my day ~~ambling~~ hiking through ~~the splendor of~~ the Appalachian Mountains.

14c Avoiding Clichés

Clichés are trite expressions that have lost all meaning because they have been so overused. Familiar sayings like "fun-filled days," "happy as a clam," and "roaring campfire," for example, are now virtually meaningless. Avoid the temptation to use clichés in your college writing. Either substitute a direct expression, or take the time to think of original, fresh language.

14d Avoiding Biased Language

(1) Offensive Labels

When referring to a racial, ethnic, or religious group, use words with neutral connotations or words that the group itself uses in *formal* speech or writing. Also avoid potentially offensive labels relating to age, class, occupation, physical ability, or sexual orientation.

(2) Sexist Language

Sexist language entails much more than the use of derogatory words such as *hunk* and *bimbo*. Assuming that some professions are exclusive to one gender—for instance, that *nurse* denotes only women or that *engineer* denotes only men—is also sexist. So is the use of job titles such as *postman* for *letter carrier* and *stewardess* for *flight attendant*.

Sexist language also occurs when a writer fails to apply the same terminology to both men and women. For example, you should refer to two scientists with PhDs not as Dr. Sagan and Mrs. Yallow, but as Dr. Sagan and Dr. Yallow.

In your writing, always use *women*—not *girls* or *ladies*—when referring to adult females. Also avoid using the generic *he* or *him* when your subject could be either male or female. Use the third-person plural or the phrase *he or she* (not *he/she*).

SEXIST: Before boarding, each passenger should make certain that <u>he</u> has <u>his</u> ticket.

REVISED: Before boarding, <u>passengers</u> should make certain that <u>they</u> have <u>their</u> tickets.

REVISED: Before boarding, each <u>passenger</u> should make certain that <u>he or she</u> has a ticket.

Remember, however, not to overuse *his or her* or *he or she* constructions, which can make your writing repetitious and wordy.

NOTE: When trying to avoid sexist use of *he* and *him*, be careful not to use *they* or *their* to refer to a singular antecedent.

Drivers
~~Any driver~~ caught speeding should have their driving privileges suspended.

✔ ELIMINATING SEXIST LANGUAGE

SEXIST USAGE	POSSIBLE REVISIONS
1. Mankind	People, human beings
Man's accomplishments	Human accomplishments
Man-made	Synthetic
2. Female doctor (lawyer, accountant, etc.), male nurse	Doctor (lawyer, accountant, etc.), nurse

continued on the following page

continued from the previous page

SEXIST USAGE	POSSIBLE REVISIONS
3. Policeman/woman Salesman/woman/girl Businessman/woman	Police officer Salesperson/representative Businessperson, executive
4. Everyone should complete his application by Tuesday.	Everyone should complete his or her application by Tuesday. All students should complete their applications by Tuesday.

PART 4

UNDERSTANDING PUNCTUATION

CHAPTER 15

END PUNCTUATION

15a Using Periods

Use a period to signal the end of most sentences, including indirect questions.

Something is rotten in Denmark.

They wondered whether the water was safe to drink.

Periods also appear in most abbreviations.

Mr. Spock	Aug.	Dr. Who
9 p.m.	etc.	221B Baker St.

If an abbreviation ends the sentence, do not add another period.

He promised to be there at 6 a.m.

However, do add a question mark if the sentence is a question.

Did he arrive at 6 p.m.?

If the abbreviation falls *within* a sentence, use normal punctuation after the period.

He promised to be there at 6 p.m., but he forgot.

 CLOSE-UP **ABBREVIATIONS WITHOUT PERIODS**

Abbreviations composed of all capital letters do not usually require periods unless they stand for initials of people's names (E. B. White).

MD   RN   BC

Familiar abbreviations of names of corporations or government agencies and scientific and technical terms do not require periods.

CD-ROM   NYU   DNA   EPA   WCAU-FM

continued on the following page

continued from the previous page

Acronyms—new words formed from the initial letters or first few letters of a series of words—do not include periods.

OSHA   AIDS   NAFTA   CAT scan

Clipped forms (commonly accepted shortened forms of words, such as *gym, dorm, math,* or *fax*) do not use a period.

15b Using Question Marks

Use a question mark to signal the end of a direct question.

Who was that masked man?

Use a question mark in parentheses to indicate that a date or number is uncertain.

Aristophanes, the Greek playwright, was born in 448 (?) BC and died in 380 (?) BC.

CLOSE-UP EDITING MISUSED QUESTION MARKS

Use a period, not a question mark, with an indirect question.

The personnel officer asked whether he knew how to type?.

Do not use a question mark to convey sarcasm. Instead, suggest your attitude through word choice.

               not very
I refused his generous (?) offer.

15c Using Exclamation Points

Use an exclamation point to signal the end of an emotional or emphatic statement, an emphatic interjection, or a forceful command.

Remember the Maine!

"No! Don't leave!," he cried.

USING EXCLAMATION POINTS

Except for recording dialogue, exclamation points are almost never appropriate in college writing. Even in informal writing, use exclamation points sparingly.

CHAPTER 16

THE COMMA

16a Setting Off Independent Clauses

Use a comma when you form a compound sentence by linking two independent clauses with a **coordinating conjunction** (*and, but, or, nor, for, yet, so*) or a pair of **correlative conjunctions**.

> The House approved the bill, <u>but</u> the Senate rejected it.

> <u>Either</u> the hard drive is full, <u>or</u> the modem is too slow.

NOTE: You may omit the comma if two clauses connected by a coordinating conjunction are very short.

> Seek and ye shall find.   Love it or leave it.

16b Setting Off Items in a Series

Use commas between items in a series of three or more coordinate elements (words, phrases, or clauses).

> <u>*Chipmunk*</u>, <u>*raccoon*</u>, and <u>*Mugwump*</u> are Native American words.

> You may pay <u>by check</u>, <u>with a credit card</u>, or <u>in cash</u>.

> <u>Brazilians speak Portuguese</u>, <u>Columbians speak Spanish</u>, and <u>Haitians speak French and Creole</u>.

NOTE: To avoid ambiguity, always use a comma before the coordinating conjunction that separates the last two items in a series.

Do not use a comma to introduce or to close a series.

> Three important criteria are⁄ fat content, salt content, and taste.

> The provinces Quebec, Ontario, and Alberta⁄are in Canada.

Use a comma between items in a series of two or more **coordinate adjectives**—adjectives that modify the same word or word group—unless they are joined by a conjunction.

She brushed her <u>long</u>, <u>shining</u> hair.

The baby was <u>tired</u> and <u>cranky</u> and <u>wet</u>.

✔ CHECKLIST: PUNCTUATING ADJECTIVES IN A SERIES

✔ If you can reverse the order of the adjectives or insert *and* between the adjectives without changing the meaning, the adjectives are coordinate, and you should use a comma.

She brushed her long , shining hair.
She brushed her shining , long hair.
She brushed her long [and] shining hair.

✔ If you cannot, the adjectives are not coordinate, and you should not use a comma.

Ten red balloons fell from the ceiling.
Red ten balloons fell from the ceiling.
Ten [and] red balloons fell from the ceiling.

16c Setting Off Introductory Elements

An introductory dependent clause, verbal phrase, or prepositional phrase is generally set off from the rest of the sentence by a comma.

<u>Although the CIA used to call undercover agents *penetration agents*</u>, they now routinely refer to them as *moles.* (dependent clause)

<u>Pushing onward</u>, Scott struggled toward the Pole. (verbal phrase)

<u>During the Depression</u>, movie attendance rose. (prepositional phrase)

If the clause or phrase is short, you may omit the comma—*provided the sentence will be clear without it.*

<u>When I exercise</u> I drink plenty of water.

<u>After the exam</u> I took a four-hour nap.

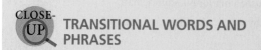

CLOSE-UP **TRANSITIONAL WORDS AND PHRASES**

When transitional words and phrases begin a sentence, they are usually set off with commas.

<u>However</u>, any plan that is enacted must be fair.

<u>In other words</u>, we cannot act hastily.

16d Setting Off Nonessential Material

Use commas to set off nonessential material whether it appears at the beginning, in the middle, or at the end of a sentence.

(1) Nonrestrictive Modifiers

Restrictive modifiers supply information essential to the meaning of the word or word group they modify and are *not* set off from it by commas. **Nonrestrictive modifiers,** which supply information not essential to the meaning of the word or word group they modify, *are* set off by commas.

Compare these two sentences.

Actors who have inflated egos are often insecure.

Actors, who have inflated egos, are often insecure.

In the first sentence, *who have inflated egos* is **restrictive;** the writer is limiting the discussion to a certain type of actor. The sentence indicates that only those actors with inflated egos—not all actors—are insecure.

In the second sentence, the modifying phrase *who have inflated egos* is **nonrestrictive.** The sentence indicates that *all* actors—not just those with inflated egos—are insecure.

As the following examples illustrate, commas set off only nonrestrictive modifiers—those that supply nonessential information—never restrictive modifiers, which supply essential information.

Adjective Clauses
RESTRICTIVE: Speaking in public is something <u>that most people fear</u>.

NONRESTRICTIVE: He ran for the bus, <u>which was late as usual</u>.

Prepositional Phrases
RESTRICTIVE: The man <u>with the gun</u> demanded their money.

NONRESTRICTIVE: The clerk, with a nod, dismissed me.

Verbal Phrases
RESTRICTIVE: The candidates <u>running for mayor</u> have agreed to a debate.

NONRESTRICTIVE: The marathoner, <u>running his fastest</u>, beat his previous record.

Appositives
RESTRICTIVE: The film <u>*Citizen Kane*</u> made Orson Welles famous.

NONRESTRICTIVE: *Citizen Kane*, <u>Orson Welles's first film</u>, made him famous.

✔ CHECKLIST: RESTRICTIVE AND NONRESTRICTIVE MODIFIERS

To determine whether a modifier is restrictive or nonrestrictive, ask these questions.

✔ Is the modifier essential to the meaning of the noun it modifies (*The man with the gun*, not just any man)? If so, it is restrictive and does not take commas.

✔ Is the modifier introduced by *that* (*something that most people fear*)? If so, it is restrictive. *That* cannot introduce a nonrestrictive clause.

✔ Can you delete the relative pronoun without causing ambiguity or confusion (*something [that] most people fear*)? If so, the clause is restrictive.

✔ Is the appositive more specific than the noun that precedes it (*the film* Citizen Kane)? If so, it is restrictive.

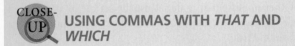

CLOSE-UP USING COMMAS WITH *THAT* AND *WHICH*

That is used to introduce only restrictive clauses; *which* can be used to introduce both restrictive and nonrestrictive clauses. Many writers, however, prefer to use *which* only to introduce nonrestrictive clauses.

See 2b

(2) Transitional Words and Phrases

<u>Transitional words and phrases</u> qualify, clarify, and make connections. However, they are not essential to meaning. For this reason, they are always set off by commas when they interrupt or come at the end of a clause.

> The Outward Bound program, <u>according to its staff</u>, is extremely safe.

> Some things were easier after school started. Other things were a lot harder, <u>however</u>.

CLOSE-UP **TRANSITIONAL WORDS AND PHRASES**

When a transitional word or phrase joins two independent clauses, it must be preceded by a semicolon and followed by a comma.

Laughter is the best medicine; <u>of course</u>, penicillin also comes in handy sometimes.

(3) Contradictory Phrases and Absolute Phrases

A phrase that expresses contrast is usually set off by commas.

> This medicine is taken after meals, <u>never on an empty stomach</u>.

> Mark McGwire, <u>not Sammy Sosa</u>, was the first to break Roger Maris's record.

An **absolute phrase,** which usually consists of a noun plus a participle, is always set off by commas from the sentence it modifies.

> <u>His fear increasing</u>, he waited to enter the haunted house.

(4) Miscellaneous Nonessential Material

Other nonessential material usually set off by commas include tag questions, names in direct address, mild interjections, and *yes* and *no*.

> This is your first day on the job, <u>isn't it</u>?

> I wonder, <u>Mr. Honeywell</u>, whether Mr. Albright deserves a raise.

> <u>Well</u>, it's about time.

> <u>Yes</u>, we have no bananas.

16e Using Commas in Other Conventional Contexts

(1) Around Direct Quotations

In most cases, use commas to set off a direct quotation from the **identifying tag** (*he said, she answered,* and so on).

Emerson said, "I greet you at the beginning of a great career."

"I greet you at the beginning of a great career," Emerson said.

"I greet you," Emerson said, "at the beginning of a great career."

When the identifying tag comes between two complete sentences, however, the tag is introduced by a comma but followed by a period.

"Winning isn't everything," Vince Lombardi said. "It's the only thing."

(2) With Titles or Degrees Following a Name

Michael Crichton, MD, wrote *Jurassic Park*.

Hamlet, Prince of Denmark, is Shakespeare's most famous character.

(3) In Dates and Addresses

On August 30, 1983, the space shuttle *Challenger* was launched.

Her address is 600 West End Avenue, New York, NY 10024.

NOTE: When only the month and year are given, no commas are used (May 1968). No comma separates the street number from the street or the state name from the zip code.

16f Using Commas to Prevent Misreading

Consider the following sentence.

Those who can, sprint the final lap.

Without the comma, *can* appears to be an auxiliary verb ("Those who can sprint. . . ."), and the sentence seems incomplete. The comma tells readers to pause, preventing confusion and ambiguity.

Also use a comma to acknowledge the omission of a repeated word, usually a verb, and to separate words repeated consecutively.

Pam carried the box; Tim, the suitcase.

Everything bad that could have happened, happened.

16g Editing Misused Commas

Do not use commas in the following situations.

(1) To Set Off Restrictive Modifiers

The film, *Malcolm X*, was directed by Spike Lee.

They planned a picnic, in the park.

(2) Between a Subject and Its Predicate

A woman with dark red hair, opened the door.

(3) Between a Verb and an Indirect Quotation

General Douglas MacArthur vowed, that he would return.

(4) Between Compounds That Are Not Independent Clauses

During the 1400s plagues, and pestilence were common. (compound subject)

Many women thirty-five and older are returning to college, and tend to be good students. (compound predicate)

(5) Before a Dependent Clause at the End of a Sentence

Jane Addams founded Hull House, because she wanted to help Chicago's poor.

CHAPTER 17

THE SEMICOLON

The **semicolon** is used only between items of equal grammatical rank: two independent clauses, two phrases, and so on.

17a Separating Independent Clauses

Use a semicolon between closely related independent clauses that convey parallel or contrasting information but are not joined by a coordinating conjunction.

Paul Revere's *The Boston Massacre* is an early example of American protest art; Edward Hick's later "primitive" paintings are socially conscious art with a religious strain.

CLOSE-UP USING SEMICOLONS

Using only a comma or no punctuation at all between independent clauses creates a <u>comma splice</u> or <u>fused sentence</u>.

See Ch. 3

Use a semicolon between two independent clauses when the second clause is introduced by a transitional word or phrase.

Thomas Jefferson brought two hundred vanilla beans and a recipe for vanilla ice cream back from France; <u>thus</u>, he gave America its all-time favorite ice cream flavor.

17b Separating Items in a Series

Use semicolons between items in a series when one or more of these items include commas.

Three papers are posted on the bulletin board outside the building: a description of the exams; a list of appeal procedures for students who fail; and an employment ad from an automobile factory, addressed specifically to candidates whose appeals are turned down. (Andrea Lee, *Russian Journal*)

Laramie, Wyoming; Wyoming, Delaware; and Delaware,
Ohio, were three of the places they visited.

17c Editing Misused Semicolons

Do not use semicolons in the following situations.

(1) Between a Dependent and an Independent Clause

Because drugs can now suppress the body's immune reaction;/fewer organ transplants are rejected.

(2) To Introduce a List

The evening news is a battleground for the three major television networks;/CBS, NBC, and ABC.

(3) To Introduce a Direct Quotation

Marie Antoinette may not have said;/"Let them eat cake."

CHAPTER 18

THE APOSTROPHE

Use an apostrophe to form the possessive case, to indicate omissions in contractions, and to form certain plurals.

18a Forming the Possessive Case

The possessive case indicates ownership. In English the possessive case of nouns and indefinite pronouns is indicated either with a phrase that includes the word *of* (the hands *of* the clock) or with an apostrophe and, in most cases, an *s* (the clock's hands).

(1) Singular Nouns and Indefinite Pronouns

To form the possessive case of singular nouns and indefinite pronouns, add -'s.

When we would arrive was anyone's guess.

NOTE: For some singular nouns that end in -s, pronouncing the possessive ending as a separate syllable can sound awkward; in such cases, it is acceptable to use just an apostrophe: Crispus Attucks' death, Aristophanes' *Lysistrata*.

(2) Plural Nouns

To form the possessive case of regular plural nouns (those that end in -s or -es), add only an apostrophe.

two weeks' severance pay and three months' medical benefits

the Lopezes' three children

To form the possessive case of nouns that have irregular plurals, add -'s.

The Children's Hour is a play by Lillian Hellman.

(3) Compound Nouns or Groups of Words

To form the possessive case of compound words or of groups of words, add -'s to the last word.

the Secretary of State's   someone else's responsibility
    resignation

(4) Two or More Items

To indicate individual ownership of two or more items, add -'s to each item.

Ernest Hemingway's and Gertrude Stein's writing styles have some similarities.

To indicate joint ownership, add -'s only to the last item.

We studied Lewis and Clark's expedition.

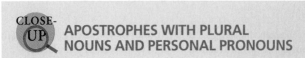

CLOSE-UP APOSTROPHES WITH PLURAL NOUNS AND PERSONAL PRONOUNS

Do not use apostrophes with plural nouns that are not possessive.

The Thompson's are out.

Do not use apostrophes to form the possessive case of personal pronouns.

This ticket must be your's or her's.

See
18b

NOTE: Be careful not to confuse <u>contractions</u> with the possessive forms of personal pronouns.

Contraction	*Possessive Form*
<u>Who's</u> on first?	<u>Whose</u> book is this?
<u>They're</u> playing our song.	<u>Their</u> team is winning.
<u>It's</u> raining.	<u>Its</u> paws were muddy.
<u>You're</u> a real pal.	<u>Your</u> résumé is very impressive.

18b Indicating Omissions in Contractions

Apostrophes replace omitted letters in contractions that combine a pronoun and a verb (*he + will = he'll*) or the elements of a verb phrase (*do + not = don't*).

FREQUENTLY USED CONTRACTIONS

it's (it is)   let's (let us)
we've (we have)   isn't (is not)

continued on the following page

---

continued from the previous page

they're (they are)	wouldn't (would not)
we'll (we will)	don't (do not)
I'm (I am)	won't (will not)

In informal writing an apostrophe may also be used to represent the century in a year: Class of '97, the '60s.

18c   Forming Plurals

In a few special situations, add -'s to form plurals.

FORMING PLURALS WITH APOSTROPHES

Plurals of Letters

The Italian language has no *j*'s or *k*'s.

Plurals of Words Referred to as Words

The supervisor would accept no *if*'s, *and*'s, or *but*'s.

NOTE:  (letters, numerals, or words) are set in italic type; the plural ending, however, is not.

See
23c

CHAPTER 19

QUOTATION MARKS

Use quotation marks to set off brief quotations (including dialogue), titles, and words used in special ways. Do not use quotation marks with long passages of prose or poetry.

19a Setting Off Quotations

When you quote a word, phrase, or brief passage from someone else's speech or writing, enclose the quoted material in a pair of quotation marks.

Gloria Steinem observed, "We are becoming the men we once hoped to marry."

"In the future," pop artist Andy Warhol once said, "everyone will be world-famous for fifteen minutes."

"Is Ankara the capital of Turkey?" she asked.

Galsworthy describes Aunt Juley as "prostrated by the blow" (329).

When you record **dialogue,** enclose the quoted words in quotation marks. Begin a new paragraph each time a new speaker is introduced.

"Sharp on time as usual," Davis said with his habitual guilty grin.

"My watch is always a little fast," Castle said, apologizing for the criticism which he had not expressed. "An anxiety complex, I suppose." (Graham Greene, *The Human Factor*)

See
20e2 **NOTE:** One line of **poetry** should be treated like a short prose passage—enclosed in quotation marks and run into the text. Two to three lines of poetry, separated by **slashes**, are also run into the text.

Do *not* enclose a **long prose passage** (more than four lines) in quotation marks. Instead, set it off by indenting the entire passage one inch (or ten spaces) from the left-hand margin. Double-space above and below the quotation, and double-space between lines within it. Introduce the passage with a colon.

The following portrait of Aunt Juley illustrates several of the devices Galsworthy uses throughout The Forsyte Saga, such as journalistic detachment, a sense of the grotesque, and irony:

> Aunt Juley stayed in her room, prostrated by the blow.
> Her face, discoloured by tears, was divided into
> compartments by the little ridges of pouting flesh
> which had swollen with emotion. . . . Her warm heart
> could not bear the thought that Ann was lying there
> so cold. (329)

Similar characterizations appear throughout the novel. . . .

NOTE: More than three lines of poetry should be set off like a long prose passage.

CLOSE-UP   LONG PROSE PASSAGES

When you quote a prose passage longer than four lines, and it is a single paragraph, do not indent the first line. When quoting two or more paragraphs, however, indent the first line of each paragraph (including the first) *three* additional spaces. If the first sentence of the passage does not begin a paragraph in the source, do not indent it.

NOTE: <u>APA guidelines</u> differ from those set forth here, which conform to MLA style.

See
A3

19b   Setting Off Titles

See
23a

<u>Titles</u> of short works and titles of parts of long works are enclosed in quotation marks. Other titles are italicized.

TITLES REQUIRING QUOTATION MARKS

Articles in Magazines, Newspapers, and Professional Journals
   "Why Johnny Can't Write" (*Newsweek*)

Essays, Short Stories, Short Poems, and Songs
   "Fenimore Cooper's Literary Offenses"
   "Flying Home"
   "The Road Not Taken"
   "The Star-Spangled Banner"

Chapters or Sections of Books
   "Miss Sharp Begins to Make Friends" (Chapter 10 of *Vanity Fair*)

continued on the following page

---

continued from the previous page
Episodes of Radio or Television Series
   "Lucy Goes to the Hospital" (*I Love Lucy*)

19c Setting Off Words Used in Special Ways

A word used in a special or unusual way is enclosed in quotation marks.

It was clear that adults approved of children who were "readers," but it was not at all clear why this was so. (Annie Dillard, *New York Times Magazine*)

A **coinage**—an invented word—also takes quotation marks.

After the twins were born, the station wagon became a "babymobile."

19d Using Quotation Marks with Other Punctuation

Quotation marks come *after* the comma or period at the end of a quotation.

Many, like Frost, think about "the road not taken," but not many have taken "the one less traveled by."

Quotation marks come *before* a semicolon or colon at the end of a quotation.

Students who do not pass the test receive "certificates of completion"; those who pass are awarded diplomas.

Taxpayers were pleased with the first of the candidate's promised "sweeping new reforms": a balanced budget.

If a question mark, exclamation point, or dash is part of the quotation, place the quotation marks *after* the punctuation.

"Who's there?" she demanded.

"Stop!" he cried.

"Should we leave now, or—" Vicki paused, unable to continue.

If a question mark, exclamation point, or dash is not part of the quotation, place the quotation marks *before* the punctuation.

Did you finish reading "The Black Cat"?

Whatever you do, don't yell "Uncle"!

The first story—Updike's "*A & P*"—provoked discussion.

QUOTATIONS WITHIN QUOTATIONS

Use single quotation marks to enclose a quotation within a quotation.

Claire noted, "Liberace always said, 'I cried all the way to the bank.'"

Also use single quotation marks within a quotation to indicate a title that would normally be enclosed in double quotation marks.

I think what she said was, "Play it, Sam. Play 'As Time Goes By.'"

Use double quotation marks around quotations or titles within a **long prose passage**.

See
19a

19e   Editing Misused or Overused Quotation Marks

Quotation marks should not be used to set off indirect quotations (someone else's written or spoken words that are not quoted exactly).

Freud wondered ~~"~~what a woman wanted.~~"~~

Do not use quotation marks to set off slang or technical terms.

Dawn is ~~"~~into~~"~~ running.

~~"~~Biofeedback~~"~~ is sometimes used to treat migraines.

TITLES OF YOUR OWN PAPERS

Do not use quotation marks to set off the title on the title page or the first page of your own papers.

CHAPTER 20

OTHER PUNCTUATION MARKS

20a Using Colons

The **colon** is a strong punctuation mark that points readers ahead to the rest of the sentence. When a colon introduces a list or series, explanatory material, or a quotation, it must be preceded by a complete independent clause.

(1) Introducing Lists or Series

Colons set off lists or series, including those introduced by phrases like *the following* or *as follows.*

> Waiting tables requires three skills : memory, speed, and balance.

(2) Introducing Explanatory Material

Colons often introduce material that explains, exemplifies, or summarizes.

> She had one dream : to play professional basketball.

Sometimes a colon separates two independent clauses, the second illustrating or clarifying the first.

> His survey reveals an interesting finding : Americans don't trust the news media.

CLOSE-UP — USING COLONS

When a complete sentence follows a colon, it may begin with either a capital or a lowercase letter. However, if it is a quotation, the first word is always capitalized (unless it was not capitalized in the source).

(3) Introducing Quotations

A quotation of more than four lines is always introduced by a colon. In addition, a colon is used before a short quotation when it is introduced by a complete independent clause.

> With dignity, Bartleby repeated the words again : "I prefer not to."

See
A4

OTHER CONVENTIONAL USES OF COLONS

To Separate Titles from Subtitles
Family Installments : *Memories of Growing Up Hispanic*

To Separate Minutes from Hours
6:15 a.m.

After Salutations in <u>Business Letters</u>
Dear Dr. Evans:

---

(4) Editing Misused Colons

Colons are not used after expressions such as *namely, for example, such as,* or *that is.*

The Eye Institute treats patients with a wide variety of conditions, such as⟋ myopia, glaucoma, and cataracts.

Colons should not be placed between verbs and their objects or complements, or between prepositions and their objects.

James Michener wrote⟋ *Hawaii, Centennial, Space,* and *Poland.*

Hitler's armies marched through⟋ the Netherlands, Belgium, and France.

20b Using Dashes

(1) Setting Off Nonessential Material

See
16d

Like commas, **dashes** can set off <u>nonessential material</u>, but unlike commas, dashes tend to call attention to the material they set off. When you type, you indicate a dash with two unspaced hyphens (unless your word processing program has a dash function).

Explanations, qualifications, examples, definitions, and appositives may be set off by dashes for emphasis or clarity.

Neither of the boys—both nine-year-olds—had any history of violence.

Too many parents learn the dangers of swimming pools the hard way—after their toddler has drowned.

(2) Introducing a Summary

A dash is used to introduce a statement that summarizes a list or series before it.

"Study hard," "Respect your elders," "Don't talk with your mouth full"——Sharon had often heard her parents say these things.

(3) Indicating an Interruption

In dialogue, a dash may mark a hesitation or an unfinished thought.

"I think——no, I know——this is the worst day of my life," Julie sighed.

(4) Editing Overused Dashes

When used to excess, dashes can make a passage seem disorganized and out of control. For this reason, dashes should not be overused.

Registration was a nightmare~~, most~~ ^{Most} of the courses I wanted to take—geology and conversational Spanish, for instance—met at inconvenient times~~or~~ were closed by the time I tried to sign up for them.

20c　Using Parentheses

(1) Setting Off Nonessential Material

Parentheses enclose material that is relatively unimportant in a sentence—for example, material that expands, clarifies, illustrates, or supplements.

In some European countries (notably Sweden and France), superb daycare is offered at little or no cost to parents.

When a complete sentence set off by parentheses falls within another sentence, it should not begin with a capital letter or end with a period.

The area is so cold (temperatures average in the low twenties) that it is virtually uninhabitable.

If the parenthetical sentence does *not* fall within another sentence, however, it must begin with a capital letter and end with appropriate punctuation.

(2) Using Parentheses in Other Situations

Parentheses are used around letters and numbers that identify points on a list, dates, cross-references, and documentation.

All reports must include the following components: (1) an opening summary, (2) a background statement, and (3) a list of conclusions.

Russia defeated Sweden in the Great Northern War (1700–1721).

Other scholars also make this point (see p. 54).

One critic has called the novel "puerile" (Arvin 72).

20d Using Brackets

Brackets within quotations tell readers that the enclosed words are yours and not those of your source. You can bracket an explanation, a clarification, a correction, or an opinion.

"Even at Princeton he [F. Scott Fitzgerald] felt like an outsider."

If a quotation contains an error, indicate that the error is not yours by following the error with the italicized Latin word *sic* ("thus") in brackets.

"The octopuss [*sic*] is a cephalopod mollusk with eight arms."

NOTE: Use brackets instead of parentheses that fall within parentheses.

CLOSE-UP USING BRACKETS

Use brackets to indicate changes that enable you to fit a **quotation** smoothly into your sentence.

See 28a1

20e Using Slashes

(1) Separating One Option from Another

The either / or fallacy is a common error in logic.

Writer / director Spike Lee will speak at the film festival.

Notice that in this case there is no space before or after the slash.

(2) Separating Lines of Poetry Run into the Text

The poet James Schevill writes, "I study my defects / And learn how to perfect them."

In this case, leave a space both before and after the slash.

20f Using Ellipses

Use an **ellipsis**—three *spaced* periods—to indicate words or entire sentences omitted from a prose quotation.

ORIGINAL: "When I was a young man, being anxious to distinguish myself, I was perpetually starting new propositions. But I soon gave this over; for I found that generally what was new was false." (Samuel Johnson)

WITH OMISSIONS: "When I was a young man, ... I was perpetually starting new propositions. But I soon ... found that generally what was new was false."

Note that when you delete words immediately after an internal punctuation mark (such as a comma), you retain the punctuation before the ellipsis.

When you delete words *at the beginning of a sentence within a quoted passage,* retain the previous sentence's punctuation, followed by an ellipsis.

In her final paragraph, Jaynes poses—and answers—her central question: "What is power? ... the option not only of saying *no* but also of saying *yes.*"

When you delete words *at the end of a sentence of a quoted passage,* retain the sentence's period or other end punctuation, followed by an ellipsis.

According to humorist Dave Barry, "from outer space Europe appears to be shaped like a large ketchup stain ..."

Similarly, if you omit *one or more complete sentences from a quoted passage,* retain the previous sentence's end punctuation, followed by an ellipsis.

NOTE: Never begin a quotation with an ellipsis. Use an ellipsis only if you delete words in the middle or at the end of a quoted passage.

CLOSE-UP USING ELLIPSES

If a quotation ending with an ellipsis is followed by parenthetical documentation, the final punctuation *follows* the documentation.

As Jarman argues, "Compromise was impossible ..." (161).

PART 5

SPELLING AND MECHANICS

CHAPTER 21

SPELLING

21a Understanding Spelling and Pronunciation

The many inconsistencies between sound and spelling in English create a number of problems. Because pronunciation provides no clues to spelling, you must memorize the spellings of many words and use a dictionary or spell checker regularly.

(1) Vowels in Unstressed Positions

Many unstressed vowels sound exactly alike when we say them. For instance, the unstressed vowels *a, e,* and *i* are impossible to distinguish by pronunciation alone in the suffixes *-able* and *-ible, -ance* and *-ence,* and *-ant* and *-ent.*

comfort<u>able</u>	brilli<u>ance</u>	serv<u>ant</u>
compat<u>ible</u>	excell<u>ence</u>	independ<u>ent</u>

(2) Silent Letters

Some English words contain silent letters, such as the *b* in *climb* and the *t* in *mortgage.*

a<u>i</u>sle	depo<u>t</u>
condem<u>n</u>	<u>k</u>night
des<u>c</u>end	<u>p</u>neumonia

(3) Words That Are Often Pronounced Carelessly

Words like the following are often misspelled because they are pronounced incorrectly.

candi<u>d</u>ate	govern<u>m</u>ent	recognize
environ<u>m</u>ent	lib<u>r</u>ary	suppose<u>d</u> to
Feb<u>r</u>uary	quan<u>t</u>ity	use<u>d</u> to

(4) Homophones

Homophones are words—such as *accept* and *except*—that are pronounced alike but spelled differently. For a list of homophones, along with their meanings and sentences illustrating their use, consult **Appendix C,** "A Glossary of Usage."

21b Learning Spelling Rules

Memorizing a few reliable spelling rules can help you overcome some of the problems caused by inconsistencies between pronunciation and spelling.

(1) The *ie/ei* Combinations

The old rule still stands: Use *i* before *e* (*belief, chief*) except after *c* (*ceiling, receive*) or when pronounced *ay*, as in *neighbor* or *weigh*. **Exceptions:** *either, neither, foreign, leisure, weird,* and *seize*. In addition, if the *ie* combination is not pronounced as a unit, the rule does not apply: *atheist, science*.

(2) Doubling Final Consonants

The only words that double their consonants before a suffix that begins with a vowel (such as *-ed* or *-ing*) are those that pass all three of the following tests.

- They have one syllable or are stressed on the last syllable.
- They have only one vowel in the last syllable.
- They end in a single consonant.

The word *tap,* for example, has only one syllable, it has only one vowel, and it ends in a single consonant, so the final consonant doubles before a suffix beginning with a vowel (*tapped, tapping*).

(3) Silent *e* before a Suffix

When a suffix that starts with a consonant is added to a word ending in a silent *e*, the *e* is generally kept: *hope/hopeful*. **Exceptions:** *argument, truly, ninth, judgment,* and *abridgment*.

When a suffix that starts with a vowel is added to a word ending in a silent *e*, the *e* is generally dropped: *hope/hoping*. **Exceptions:** *changeable, noticeable,* and *courageous*.

(4) *y* before a Suffix

When a word ends in a consonant plus *y*, the *y* generally changes to an *i* when a suffix is added (*beauty + ful = beautiful*). The *y* is retained, however, when the suffix *-ing* is added (*tally + ing = tallying*) and in some one-syllable words (*dry + ness = dryness*).

When a word ends in a vowel plus *y*, the *y* is retained (*joy + ful = joyful*). **Exception:** *day + ly = daily*.

(5) *seed* Endings

Endings with the sound *seed* are nearly always spelled *cede*, as in *precede*. **Exceptions:** *supersede, exceed, proceed,* and *succeed*.

(6) *-able, -ible*

If the root of a word is itself an independent word, the suffix *-able* is most commonly used (*comfortable, agreeable*). If the root of a word is not an independent word, the suffix *-ible* is most often used (*compatible, incredible*).

(7) Plurals

Most nouns form plurals by adding *-s: tortilla/tortillas, boat/boats.* There are, however, a number of exceptions.

Some words ending in *-f* or *-fe* form plurals by changing the *f* to *v* and adding *-es* or *-s: life/lives, self/selves.* Others add just *-s: belief/beliefs, safe/safes.*

Most words that end in a consonant followed by *y* form plurals by changing the *y* to *i* and adding *-es: baby/babies.* **Exceptions:** proper nouns such as *Kennedy* (plural *Kennedys*).

Most words that end in a consonant followed by *o* add *-es* to form the plural: *tomato/tomatoes, hero/heroes.* **Exceptions:** *silo/silos, piano/pianos, memo/memos, soprano/sopranos.*

Words ending in *-s, -sh, -ch, -x,* and *-z* form plurals by adding *-es: Jones/Joneses, rash/rashes, lunch/lunches, box/boxes, buzz/buzzes.*

NOTE: Some one-syllable words that end in *-s* or *-z* double their final consonants when forming plurals: *quiz/quizzes.*

In hyphenated compound nouns whose first element is more important than the others, the plural is formed with the first element: *sister-in-law/sisters-in-law.*

Some words, especially those borrowed from Latin or Greek, keep their foreign plurals.

Singular	Plural
criterion	criteria
larva	larvae
memorandum	memoranda
stimulus	stimuli

RUNNING A SPELL CHECK

If you use a computer spell checker, remember that it will not identify a word that is spelled correctly but used incorrectly—*then* for *than* or *its* for *it's,* for example—or a typo that creates another word, such as *form* for *from.* Even after running a spell check, you still need to proofread your papers .

CHAPTER 22

CAPITALIZATION

In addition to capitalizing the first word of a sentence (including a quoted sentence) and the pronoun *I*, always capitalize proper nouns and important words in titles.

22a Capitalizing Proper Nouns

Proper nouns—the names of specific persons, places, or things—are capitalized, and so are adjectives formed from proper nouns.

(1) Specific People's Names

Eleanor Roosevelt   Elvis Presley

Capitalize a title when it precedes a person's name or replaces the name (Senator Barbara Boxer, Dad). Titles that *follow* names or that refer to the general position, not to the particular person who holds it, are usually not capitalized (Barbara Boxer, the senator), except for very high-ranking positions: President of the United States.

Capitalize titles or abbreviations of academic degrees, even when they follow a name: Dr. Benjamin Spock, Benjamin Spock, M.D.

(2) Names of Particular Things

the *Titanic*   the World Series
the Brooklyn Bridge   Mount Rushmore

(3) Places and Geographical Regions

Saturn   the Straits of Magellan
Budapest   the Western Hemisphere

Capitalize *north, east, south,* and *west* when they denote particular geographical regions (the West), but not when they designate directions (west of town).

(4) Days of the Week, Months, and Holidays

Saturday   Rosh Hashanah
January   Kwanzaa

(5) Historical Periods, Events, Movements, and Documents

the Reformation   Romanticism
the Battle of Gettysburg   the Treaty of Versailles

(6) Races, Ethnic Groups, Nationalities, and Languages

African-American   Korean
Latino/Latina   Dutch

NOTE: When the words *black* and *white* refer to races, they have traditionally not been capitalized. Current usage is divided on whether to capitalize *black*.

(7) Religions, Their Followers, and Sacred Terms

Jews   the Talmud   Buddha
Islam   God   the Scriptures

(8) Specific Organizations

the New York Yankees   the American Bar Association
the Democratic Party   the Anti-Defamation League

(9) Businesses, Government Agencies, and Other Institutions

Congress   Lincoln High School
the Environmental Protection   the University of
  Agency   Maryland

(10) Trade Names and Words Formed from Them

Coke   Astroturf   Rollerblades

(11) Specific Academic Courses and Departments

Sociology 201   Department of English

NOTE: Do not capitalize a general subject area (sociology, zoology) unless it is the name of a language (French).

(12) Adjectives Formed from Proper Nouns

Keynesian economics   Elizabethan era
Freudian slip   Shakespearean sonnet

When words derived from proper nouns have lost their specialized meanings, do not capitalize them: *china* pattern, *french* fries.

22b Capitalizing Important Words in Titles

In general, capitalize all words in titles with the exception of articles (*a, an,* and *the*), prepositions, coordinating conjunctions, and the *to* in infinitives. If an article, preposition, or coordinating conjunction is the *first* or *last* word in the title, however, do capitalize it.

The Declaration of Independence   *A Man and a Woman*
Across the River and into the Trees   *What Friends Are For*

CHAPTER 23

ITALICS

23a Setting Off Titles and Names

Use italics for the titles and names in the box below. All other titles are set off with **quotation marks**.

See 19b

TITLES AND NAMES SET IN ITALICS

BOOKS: *David Copperfield, The Bluest Eye*

NEWSPAPERS: the *Washington Post,* the *Philadelphia Inquirer*

(Articles and names of cities are italicized only when they are part of a title.)

MAGAZINES: *Rolling Stone, Scientific American*

PAMPHLETS: *Common Sense*

FILMS: *Casablanca, Schindler's List*

TELEVISION PROGRAMS: *60 Minutes, Beverly Hills 90210, The X-Files*

RADIO PROGRAMS: *All Things Considered, A Prairie Home Companion*

LONG POEMS: *John Brown's Body, The Faerie Queen*

PLAYS: *Macbeth, A Raisin in the Sun*

LONG MUSICAL WORKS: *Rigoletto, Eroica*

SOFTWARE PROGRAMS: *Word, PowerPoint*

PAINTINGS AND SCULPTURE: *Guernica, Pietà*

SHIPS: *Lusitania,* U.S.S. *Saratoga*

(S.S. and U.S.S. are not italicized.)

TRAINS: *City of New Orleans, The Orient Express*

AIRCRAFT: *The Hindenburg, Enola Gay*

(Only particular aircraft, not makes or types such as Piper Cub or Boeing 757, are italicized.)

SPACECRAFT: *Challenger, Enterprise*

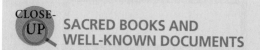

CLOSE-UP

SACRED BOOKS AND WELL-KNOWN DOCUMENTS

Names of sacred books, such as the Bible, and well-known documents, such as the Constitution and the Declaration of Independence, are neither italicized nor placed within quotation marks.

23b Setting Off Foreign Words and Phrases

Italics are often used to set off foreign words and phrases that have not become part of the English language.

"*C'est la vie,*" Madeleine said when she noticed the new, lower price.

Spirochaeta plicatilis is a corkscrew-like bacterium.

If you are not sure whether a foreign word has been assimilated into English, consult a dictionary.

23c Setting Off Elements Spoken of as Themselves and Terms Being Defined

Italics are used to set off letters, numerals, and words that refer to the letters, numerals, and words themselves.

Is that a *p* or a *g*?

I forget the exact address, but I know it has a *3* in it.

Does *through* rhyme with *cough*?

Italics also set off words and phrases that you go on to define.

A *closet drama* is a play meant to be read, not performed.

23d Using Italics for Emphasis

Italics can occasionally be used for emphasis.

Initially, poetry might be defined as a kind of language that says *more* and says it *more intensely* than does ordinary language. (Lawrence Perrine, *Sound and Sense*)

Overuse of italics is distracting. Try to indicate emphasis with word choice and sentence structure.

USING ITALICS

MLA style recommends that you underline to indicate italics. However, you may italicize if your instructor gives you permission to do so.

CHAPTER 24

HYPHENS

Hyphens have two conventional uses: to break a word at the end of a typed or handwritten line and to link words in certain compounds.

24a Breaking a Word at the End of a Line

A computer never breaks a word at the end of a line unless you command it to. Sometimes you will want to hyphenate—for example, to fill in space at the end of a line. When you break a word at the end of a line, divide it only between syllables, consulting a dictionary if necessary. Never divide a word at the end of a page, and never hyphenate one-syllable words. In addition, never leave a single letter at the end of a line or carry only one or two letters to the beginning of a new line.

See
24b

If you must divide a **compound word** at the end of a line, put the hyphen between the elements of the compound (*snowmobile*, not *snowmo-bile*).

DIVIDING ELECTRONIC ADDRESSES

Do not use a hyphen when dividing a long electronic address at the end of a line. (A hyphen at this point could confuse readers, making them think it is part of the address.) Instead, simply break the address in a logical place—before or after a slash or a period, for example—or avoid the problem entirely by putting the entire address on one line.

24b Dividing Compound Words

A **compound word** is composed of two or more words. Some familiar compound words are always hyphenated: *no-hitter, helter-skelter.* Your dictionary can tell you whether a particular compound requires a hyphen.

Hyphens are generally used in the following compounds.

(1) In Compound Adjectives

When a **compound adjective** *precedes* the noun it modifies, its elements are joined by hyphens.

> The research team tried to use <u>nineteenth-century</u> technology to design a <u>space-age</u> project.

When a compound adjective *follows* the noun it modifies, it does not include hyphens.

> The three government-operated programs were run smoothly, but the one that was not <u>government operated</u> was short of funds.

 USING HYPHENS

A compound adjective formed with an adverb ending in *-ly* is not hyphenated, even when it precedes the noun.

> Many <u>upwardly mobile</u> families are on tight budgets.

(2) With Certain Prefixes or Suffixes

Use a hyphen between a prefix and a proper noun or adjective.

> mid-July   pre-Columbian

Use a hyphen to connect the prefixes *all-*, *ex-*, *half-*, *quarter-*, *quasi-*, and *self-* and the suffix *-elect* to a noun.

> ex-senator   self-centered
> quarter-moon   president-elect

Also hyphenate to avoid certain hard-to-read combinations, such as two *i*'s (*semi-illiterate*) or more than two of the same consonant (*shell-less*).

(3) In Compound Numerals and Fractions

Hyphenate compounds that represent numbers below one hundred, even if they are part of a larger number.

> the <u>twenty-first</u> century   three hundred <u>sixty-five</u> days

Also hyphenate the written form of a fraction when it modifies a noun.

> a <u>two-thirds</u> share of the business

CHAPTER 25

ABBREVIATIONS

Many **abbreviations** are not appropriate in college writing. Others are acceptable in scientific, technical, or business writing, or only in a particular discipline. If you have questions, check a style manual in your field.

25a Abbreviating Titles

Titles before and after proper names are usually abbreviated.

Mr. Homer Simpson   Rep. Chaka Fattah
Henry Kissinger, PhD   Dr. Martin Luther King, Jr.

Do not, however, use an abbreviated title without a name.

The ~~Dr.~~ doctor diagnosed hepatitis.

25b Abbreviating Organization Names and Technical Terms

See 15a

Well-known businesses and government, social, and civic organizations are commonly referred to by capitalized initials. These **abbreviations** fall into two categories: those that pronounce the initials as separate units (MTV) and **acronyms,** in which the initials form new words (NATO).

You may use accepted abbreviations for terms that are not well known, but be sure to spell out the full term the first time you mention it, followed by the abbreviation in parentheses.

Citrus farmers have been using ethylene dibromide (EDB), a chemical pesticide, for more than twenty years. Now, however, EDB has contaminated water supplies.

25c Abbreviating Dates, Times of Day, Temperatures, and Numbers

50 BC (BC follows the date)   AD 432 (AD precedes the date)
3:03 p.m. (lowercase)   180° F (Fahrenheit)

Always capitalize BC and AD. (The alternatives BCE, for "before the Common Era," and CE, for "Common Era," are also capitalized.)

The abbreviations a.m. and p.m. are used only when they are accompanied by numbers.

I'll see you in the ~~a.m.~~ morning.

Avoid the abbreviation *no.* except in technical writing, and then use it only before a specific number: *The unidentified substance was labeled no. 52.*

25d Editing Misused Abbreviations

In college writing, abbreviations are not used in the following cases.

(1) Names of Days, Months, or Holidays

On ~~Sat., Dec.~~ Saturday, December 23, I started my ~~Xmas~~ Christmas shopping.

(2) Names of Places, Streets, and the Like

He lives on Riverside ~~Dr.~~ Drive in ~~NYC~~ New York City.

Exceptions: The abbreviation *US* is often acceptable (*US Coast Guard*), as is *DC* in *Washington, DC.*

(3) Names of People and Academic Subjects

Mr. Harris's boys were named ~~Robt.~~ Robert and ~~Wm.~~ William.

~~Psych.~~ Psychology and English ~~lit.~~ literature are required courses.

(4) Units of Measurement

In technical writing, some units of measurement are abbreviated when preceded by a numeral.

The hurricane had winds of 35 mph.

One new Honda gets over 50 mpg.

In general, however, write out such expressions and spell out words such as *inches, feet, years, miles, pints, quarts,* and *gallons.*

(5) Symbols

The symbols %, =, +, #, and ¢ are acceptable in technical and scientific writing but not in nontechnical college writing. The symbol $ is acceptable before specific numbers ($15,000), but not as a substitute for the words *money* or *dollars.*

CHAPTER 26

NUMBERS

Convention determines when to use a **numeral** (22) and when to spell out a number (twenty-two). Numerals are commonly used in scientific and technical writing and in journalism, but less so in academic or literary writing.

NOTE: The guidelines in this chapter are based on the *MLA Handbook for Writers of Research Papers*. APA style requires that all numbers below ten be spelled out if they do not represent specific measurements, and that numbers ten and above be expressed in numerals.

26a Spelled-Out Numbers versus Numerals

Unless a number falls into one of the categories listed in **26b,** spell it out if you can do so *in one or two words*.

The Hawaiian alphabet has only <u>twelve</u> letters.

Class size stabilized at <u>twenty-eight</u> students.

The subsidies are expected to total about <u>two million</u> dollars.

Numbers *more than two words* long are expressed in figures.

The dietitian prepared <u>125</u> sample menus.

The developer of the community purchased <u>300,000</u> doorknobs, <u>153,000</u> faucets, and <u>4,000</u> manhole covers.

NOTE: Numerals and spelled-out numbers should generally not be mixed in the same passage. For consistency, then, the number 4,000 in the preceding example is expressed in figures even though it could be written in just two words.

Never begin a sentence with a numeral. If necessary, reword the sentence.

FAULTY: 250 students are currently enrolled in World History 106.

REVISED: Current enrollment in World History 106 is 250 students.

26b Conventional Uses of Numerals

- **Addresses:** 111 Fifth Avenue, New York, NY 10003
- **Dates:** January 15, 1929   1914–1919
- **Exact Times:** 9:16   10 a.m. or 10:00 a.m. (*but* ten o'clock)
- **Exact Sums of Money:** $25.11 $6,752.00
- **Divisions of Works:** Act 5   lines 17–28   page 42
- **Percentages:** 80 percent (or 80%)
- **Decimals and Fractions:** 3.14   6¾
- **Measurements with Symbols or Abbreviations:** 32°   15 cc
- **Ratios and Statistics:** 20 to 1   average age of 40
- **Scores:** a lead of 6 to 0
- **Identification Numbers:** Route 66   Track 8   Channel 12

PART 6

WRITING WITH SOURCES

CHAPTER 27

WRITING RESEARCH PAPERS

When you undertake a research project, you become involved in a process that requires you to think critically, evaluating and interpreting the ideas explored in your sources and formulating ideas of your own.

✔ CHECKLIST: THE RESEARCH PROCESS

- ✔ Choose a topic **(See 27a)**
- ✔ Do exploratory research and focus on a research question **(See 27b)**
- ✔ Assemble a working bibliography **(See 27c)**
- ✔ Do focused research and take notes **(See 27d)**
- ✔ Outline your paper **(See 27e1)**
- ✔ Draft your paper **(See 27e2)**
- ✔ Revise your paper **(See 27e3)**

27a Choosing a Topic

The first step in the research process is finding a topic to write about.

✔ CHECKLIST: CHOOSING A RESEARCH TOPIC

- ✔ **Are you genuinely interested in your research topic?** Be sure the topic you select is one that will hold your interest.
- ✔ **Is your topic suitable for research?** Be sure your paper will not depend on your personal experiences or value judgments.
- ✔ **Is your topic too broad? too narrow?** Be sure the boundaries of your research topic are appropriate.
- ✔ **Can your topic be researched in a library to which you have access?** Be sure your school library has the sources you need (or that you can access those sources on the Internet).

27b Doing Exploratory Research and Focusing on a Research Question

Doing **exploratory research**—looking through general reference works like encyclopedias, bibliographies, and specialized dictionaries—helps you to get an overview of your topic and an understanding of its possibilities. Your goal is to formulate a **research question,** the question you want your research paper to answer. A research question helps you to decide which sources to seek out, which to examine first, which to examine in depth, and which to skip entirely. The answer to your research question will be your paper's **thesis statement**.

See
1c

27c Assembling a Working Bibliography

As you assess the value of potential sources for your paper, be sure to record complete bibliographic information: author, title, page numbers, and complete publication information. You can enter this information either on individual index cards or in a separate computer file designated "Bibliography." (See Figures 1 and 2.) Also keep records of interviews and other non-print sources of information, as well as of sources you access through the Internet. Your note should include a brief evaluation of the kind of information each source contains, the amount of information offered, its relevance to your topic, and its limitations.

Figure 1   Information for Working Bibliography (on index card)

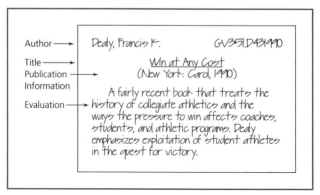

Author ⟶ Dealy, Francis K.   GV351.D431990

Title ⟶ *Win at Any Cost*
Publication ⟶ (New York: Carol, 1990)
Information

Evaluation ⟶ A fairly recent book that treats the history of collegiate athletics and the ways the pressure to win affects coaches, students, and athletic programs. Dealy emphasizes exploitation of student athletes in the quest for victory.

Figure 2 Information for Working Bibliography (in computer file)

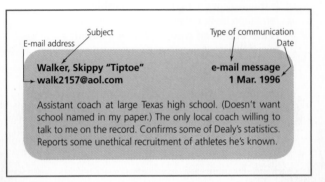

CHECKLIST: EVALUATING SOURCES

- ✔ **How relevant is your source to your needs?** How detailed is its treatment of your subject? Is your topic a major focus of your source?
- ✔ **How current is your source?** Have recent developments made any parts of your source dated? Does your source rely on information from earlier works?
- ✔ **How reliable is your source?** Is your source largely fact or opinion? Are its opinions based on fact? Is the supporting evidence accurate? Does the writer present enough evidence to support his or her position? Does the writer select representative examples? Does the author of your source reveal any bias? How respected is your source? Do other scholars mention your source in their work?

CHECKLIST: EVALUATING INTERNET SOURCES

- ✔ **Where does the information come from?** An article, for example, may be from a scholarly source, or it may be the personal opinion of an author with no expertise in the area he or she is discussing.
- ✔ **Is the sponsoring institution reputable?** Can you trust the institution to be fair and impartial?

continued on the following page

continued from the previous page

✔ **Is the author trying to sell something?** Is the information biased, slanted, or intentionally misleading?

✔ **Is the text itself credible?** Does it include evidence to support its claims? If authorities are quoted or paraphrased, does the text supply information about the credentials of the authorities?

✔ **Do slick graphics, sound, or video connected to a Web page mask uninformed opinion or faulty logic?** Don't be misled by technologically sophisticated sites that do not offer you any way to evaluate the accuracy of the information presented.

27d Doing Focused Research and Taking Notes

When you do **focused research,** you look for the specific information—facts, examples, statistics, definitions, quotations—you need to support your ideas. As you take notes, your goal is flexibility: you want to be able to arrange and rearrange information easily and efficiently. If you take notes by hand, use one index card for each piece of information rather than jotting comments down in the margins of photocopied pages or running

Figure 3 Note (on note card)

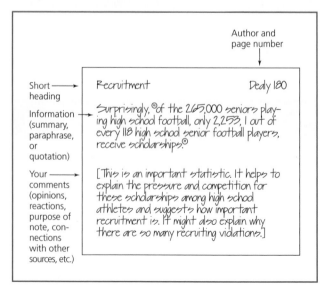

Author and page number ↓

Short heading →

Information (summary, paraphrase, or quotation) →

Your comments (opinions, reactions, purpose of note, connections with other sources, etc.) →

> Recruitment   Deely 180
>
> Surprisingly, ®of the 265,000 seniors play-ing high school football, only 2,253, 1 out of every 118 high school senior football players, receive scholarships.®
>
> [This is an important statistic. It helps to explain the pressure and competition for these scholarships among high school athletes and suggests how important recruitment is. It might also explain why there are so many recruiting violations.]

Figure 4 Note (in computer file)

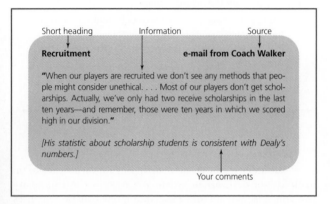

Short heading   Information   Source

Recruitment   **e-mail from Coach Walker**

"When our players are recruited we don't see any methods that people might consider unethical. . . . Most of our players don't get scholarships. Actually, we've only had two receive scholarships in the last
ten years—and remember, those were ten years in which we scored
high in our division."

*[His statistic about scholarship students is consistent with Dealy's
numbers.]*

Your comments

several ideas together on a single card. (If you take notes on a
computer, type each piece of information under a specific heading on a separate page.)

Each piece of information you record (in the form of **summary, paraphrase,** or **quotation**) should be accompanied by a
short descriptive heading that indicates its relevance to some aspect of your topic as well as by comments that make clear your
rationale for recording the information and identify what you
think it will add to your paper. Be sure to identify the source of
the information. (See Figures 3 and 4.)

✔ CHECKLIST: TAKING NOTES

- ✔ **Identify the source of each piece of information
  clearly and completely**—even if the source is sitting on your bookshelf or stored in your computer's
  hard drive.
- ✔ **Include everything now that you will need later**
  to understand your note—names, dates, places,
  connections with other notes—and to remember
  why you recorded it.
- ✔ **Distinguish quotations from paraphrases and
  summaries and your own ideas from those of
  your sources.** If you copy a source's words, place
  them in quotation marks. (If you take notes by hand,
  circle the quotation marks; if you type your notes,
  boldface the quotation marks.) If you write down your
  own ideas, bracket them and, if you are taking notes
  on a computer, italicize them as well. (Sometimes an

continued on the following page

continued from the previous page
> entire entry may record your own thoughts; if this is
> the case, bracket the complete entry.)
> ✔ **Put an author's comments into your own words**
> **whenever possible,** summarizing and paraphrasing
> material as well as adding your own observations
> and analysis.

(1) Writing a Summary

A **summary** is a brief restatement in your own words of the
main idea of a passage or article. When you write a summary,
you condense the author's ideas into a few concise sentences.
You do *not* include your own opinions or interpretations of the
writer's ideas.

Original Source

Today, the First Amendment faces challenges from
groups who seek to limit expressions of racism and bigotry.
A growing number of legislatures have passed rules against
"hate speech"—[speech] that is offensive on the basis of
race, ethnicity, gender, or sexual orientation. The rules are
intended to promote respect for all people and protect the
targets of hurtful words, gestures, or actions.

Legal experts fear these rules may wind up diminishing
the rights of all citizens. "The bedrock principle [of our so-
ciety] is that government may never suppress free speech
simply because it goes against what the community would
like to hear," says Nadine Strossen, president of the American Civil Liberties Union and professor of constitutional
law at New York University Law School. In recent years, for
example, the courts have upheld the right of neo-Nazis to
march in Jewish neighborhoods; protected cross-burning as
a form of free expression; and allowed protesters to burn
the American flag. The offensive, ugly, distasteful, or repug-
nant nature of expression is not reason enough to ban it,
courts have said.

But advocates of limits on hate speech note that certain
kinds of expression fall outside of First Amendment protection. Courts have ruled that "fighting words"—words intended to provoke immediate violence—or speech that
creates a clear and present danger are not protected forms of
expression. As the classic argument goes, freedom of speech
does not give you the right to yell "Fire!" in a crowded theater. (Sudo, Phil. "Freedom of Hate Speech?" *Scholastic Up-
date* 124.14 [1992]: 17–20.)

Summary

The right to freedom of speech, guaranteed by the First Amendment, is becoming more difficult to defend. Some people think stronger laws against the use of "hate speech" weaken the First Amendment, but others argue that some kinds of speech remain exempt from this protection (Sudo 17).

✔ CHECKLIST: WRITING A SUMMARY

✔ Write a one-sentence restatement of the main idea.
✔ Write your summary, using the one-sentence restatement as your topic sentence. Use your own words and phrasing, not those of your source. Include quotation marks where necessary.
✔ Add appropriate documentation.

---

(2) Writing a Paraphrase

A summary conveys just the essence of a source; a **paraphrase** is a *detailed* restatement in your own words of all a source's important ideas—but not your opinions of those ideas. A paraphrase not only indicates the source's main points, but it also reflects its order, tone, and emphasis. Consequently, it can sometimes be as long as the source itself. Try not to look at the source as you paraphrase—use language and syntax that come naturally to you, and avoid duplicating the wording or sentence structure of the original. If you cannot think of a synonym for an important term, quote it.

Compare the following paraphrase with the summary of the same source above.

Paraphrase

Many groups want to limit the right of free speech guaranteed by the First Amendment to the Constitution. They believe this is necessary to protect certain groups of people from "hate speech." Women, people of color, and gay men and lesbians, for example, may find that hate speech is used to intimidate them. Legal scholars are afraid that even though the rules against hate speech are well intentioned, such rules undermine our freedom of speech. As Nadine Strossen, president of the American Civil Liberties Union, says, "The bedrock principle [of our society] is that government may never suppress free speech simply because it goes against what the community would like to hear" (qtd. in Sudo 17). People who support speech codes point out, however, that certain types of speech are not protected by the First Amendment—for example, words that create a "clear and present danger" or that would lead directly to violence (Sudo 17).

✔ CHECKLIST: WRITING A PARAPHRASE

- ✔ Outline your source if necessary.
- ✔ Write your paraphrase, following the order, tone, and emphasis of the original and making sure that you do not use the words or phrasing of the original without enclosing the borrowed material within quotation marks.
- ✔ Add appropriate documentation.

(3) Recording Quotations

When you **quote,** you copy an author's remarks exactly as they appear in a source, word for word and punctuation mark for punctuation mark, enclosing the borrowed words in quotation marks. (As a rule, you should not quote extensively in a research paper. The use of numerous quotations interrupts the flow of your discussion and gives readers the impression that your paper is just an unassimilated collection of other people's ideas.)

CLOSE-UP   WHEN TO QUOTE

- Quote when a source's wording or phrasing is so distinctive that a summary or paraphrase would diminish its impact.
- Quote when a source's words—particularly those of a recognized expert on your subject—will lend authority to your paper.
- Quote when paraphrasing would create a long, clumsy, or incoherent phrase or would change the meaning of the original.
- Quote when you plan to disagree with a source. Using a source's exact words helps to assure readers you are being fair.

27e   Outlining, Drafting, and Revising

After you have finished your focused research and note taking, you will go on to develop a **thesis,** a carefully worded statement that expresses a conclusion that your research can support.

(1) Outlining

At this point, you may prepare a formal outline that indicates both the order in which you will present your ideas and the relationship of main ideas to supporting details. (Formal outlines conform to specific conventions of structure, content, and style; an excerpt from a formal outline appears at the beginning of the sample research paper on page 143.)

(2) Drafting

When you are ready to write your **rough draft**, arrange your notes in the order in which you intend to use them. Follow your outline as you write, using your notes as needed.

See 1d1

To make it easy for you to revise later on, triple-space your draft. Be careful to copy source information fully and accurately on this and every subsequent draft, placing the documentation as close as possible to the material it identifies.

(3) Revising

A good way to start revising is to check to see that your thesis statement still accurately expresses your paper's central focus. Then, make an outline of your draft, and compare it with the outline you made before you began the draft. If you find significant differences, you will have to revise your thesis statement or rewrite sections of your paper. The checklists in **1d2** can guide your revision of your paper's overall structure and its individual paragraphs, sentences, and words.

✔ CHECKLIST: REVISING A RESEARCH PAPER

- ✔ Should you do more research to find support for certain points?
- ✔ Do you need to reorder the major sections of your paper?
- ✔ Should you rearrange the order in which you present your points within those sections?
- ✔ Do you need to add section headings? Transitional paragraphs?
- ✔ Have you **integrated your notes** smoothly into your paper?

See 28a

- ✔ Do you introduce source material with **running acknowledgments**?

See 28a1

- ✔ Are quotations blended with paraphrase, summary, and your own observations and reactions?
- ✔ Have you avoided **plagiarism** by carefully documenting all borrowed ideas?

See 28b

- ✔ Have you analyzed and interpreted the ideas of others rather than simply stringing those ideas together?

continued on the following page

continued from the previous page

✔ Do your own ideas—not those of your sources—define the focus of your discussion?

See
1e

✔ Have you **edited and proofread** carefully?

✔ Have you given your paper an appropriate title?

CHAPTER 28

INTEGRATING SOURCES AND AVOIDING PLAGIARISM

28a Integrating Your Notes into Your Writing

Weave paraphrases, summaries, and quotations smoothly into your paper, adding analysis or explanation to make your discussion coherent and to show why you are using each source.

CLOSE-UP

INTEGRATING YOUR NOTES INTO YOUR WRITING

To avoid monotonous sentence structure, experiment with different methods of integrating source material into your paper.

- Vary the verbs you use to introduce a source's words or ideas (rather than always using *says*).

acknowledges	discloses	implies
suggests	observes	notes
concludes	believes	comments
insists	explains	claims
predicts	summarizes	illustrates
reports	finds	proposes
warns	concurs	speculates
admits	affirms	indicates

- Vary the placement of the **identifying tag** (the phrase that identifies the source), putting it in the middle or at the end of the quoted material instead of always at the beginning.

QUOTATION WITH IDENTIFYING TAG IN MIDDLE: "A serious problem confronting Amish society from the viewpoint of the Amish themselves," observes Hostetler,

continued on the following page

continued from the previous page

"is the threat of absorption into mass society through the values promoted in the public school system" (193).

PARAPHRASE WITH IDENTIFYING TAG AT END: The Amish are also concerned about their children's exposure to the public school system's values, notes Hostetler (193).

(1) Integrating Quotations

Quotations should never be awkwardly dropped into the paper, leaving the exact relationship between the quotation and the writer's point unclear. Instead, use a brief introductory remark to provide a context for the quotation.

UNACCEPTABLE: For the Amish, the public school system represents a problem. "A serious problem confronting Amish society from the viewpoint of the Amish themselves is the threat of absorption into mass society through the values promoted in the public school system" (Hostetler 193).

ACCEPTABLE: For the Amish, the public school system is a problem because it represents "the threat of absorption into mass society" (Hostetler 193).

Whenever possible, use a **running acknowledgment** to help readers keep track of the source of the quotation.

RUNNING ACKNOWLEDGMENT: <u>As John Hostetler points out,</u> the Amish see the public school system as a problem because it represents "the threat of absorption into mass society" (193).

Substitutions or Additions within Quotations When you make changes or additions to make a quotation fit into your paper, acknowledge your changes by enclosing them in brackets.

ORIGINAL QUOTATION: "Immediately after her wedding, she and her husband followed tradition and went to visit almost everyone who attended the wedding" (Hostetler 122).

QUOTATION REVISED TO SUPPLY AN ANTECEDENT FOR A PRONOUN: "Immediately after her wedding, [Sarah] and her husband followed tradition and went to visit almost everyone who attended the wedding" (Hostetler 122).

QUOTATION REVISED TO CHANGE A CAPITAL TO A LOWERCASE LETTER: The strength of the Amish community is illustrated by the fact that "[i]mmediately after her wedding, she and her husband followed tradition and went

to visit almost everyone who attended the wedding"
(Hostetler 122).

Omissions within Quotations   When you delete unnecessary
or irrelevant words, substitute an **ellipsis** (three spaced periods). See
20f

ORIGINAL: "Not only have the Amish built and staffed their
own elementary and vocational schools, but they have grad-
ually organized on local, state, and national levels to cope
with the task of educating their children" (Hostetler 206).

**QUOTATION REVISED TO ELIMINATE UNNECESSARY
WORDS:** "Not only have the Amish built and staffed their
own elementary and vocational schools, but they have grad-
ually organized . . . to cope with the task of educating their
children" (Hostetler 206).

CLOSE-UP   OMISSIONS WITHIN QUOTATIONS

Be sure that you do not misrepresent quoted material
when you shorten it. For example, do not say, "the Amish
have managed to maintain . . . their culture" when the
original quotation is "the Amish have managed to maintain *parts of* their culture."

For treatment of long quotations, see **19a.**

(2) Integrating Paraphrases and Summaries

Introduce your paraphrases and summaries with running
acknowledgments, and end them with appropriate documentation. Doing so allows your readers to differentiate your own
ideas from the ideas of your sources.

**MISLEADING (IDEAS OF SOURCE BLEND WITH IDEAS OF
WRITER):**   Art can be used to uncover many problems that
children have at home, in school, or with their friends. For this
reason, many therapists use art therapy extensively. Children's
views of themselves in society are often reflected by their art
style. For example, a cramped, crowded art style using only a
portion of the paper shows their limited role (Alschuler 260).

**REVISED WITH RUNNING ACKNOWLEDGMENT (IDEAS OF
SOURCE DIFFERENTIATED FROM IDEAS OF WRITER):**   Art
can be used to uncover many problems that children have at
home, in school, or with their friends. For this reason, many
therapists use art therapy extensively. According to William
Alschuler in *Art and Self-Image,* children's views of themselves in society are often reflected by their art style. For

example, a cramped, crowded art style using only a portion of the paper shows their limited role (260).

28b Avoiding Plagiarism

See
Pt. 7

Plagiarism is presenting another person's words or ideas—either accidentally or intentionally—as if they are your own. In general, you must provide **documentation** for all direct quotations, as well as for every opinion, judgment, and insight of someone else that you summarize or paraphrase. You must also document tables, graphs, charts, and statistics taken from a source.

Common knowledge, information that is generally known and that can be found in a number of general reference sources, need not be documented. Information that is in dispute or that is one person's original contribution, however, must be acknowledged. You need not, for example, document the fact that John F. Kennedy graduated from Harvard in 1940 or that he was elected president in 1960. You must, however, document a historian's analysis of Kennedy's performance as president or a researcher's recent discoveries about his private life.

You can avoid plagiarism by using documentation wherever it is required and by following these guidelines.

(1) Enclose Borrowed Words in Quotation Marks

ORIGINAL: DNA profiling begins with the established theory that no two people, except identical twins, have the same genetic makeup. Each cell in the body contains a complete set of genes. (Tucker, William. "DNA in Court." *The American Spectator* Nov. 1994: 26)

PLAGIARISM: William Tucker points out that DNA profiling is based on the premise that genetic makeup differs from person to person and that <u>each cell in the body contains a complete set of genes</u> (26).

The preceding passage does cite the source, but it irresponsibly uses the source's exact words without placing them in quotation marks.

CORRECT (BORROWED WORDS IN QUOTATION MARKS): William Tucker points out that DNA profiling is based on the premise that genetic makeup differs from person to person and that <u>"[e]ach cell in the body contains a complete set of genes"</u> (26).

CORRECT (PARAPHRASE): William Tucker points out that DNA profiling is based on the accepted premise that genetic makeup differs from person to person and that <u>every cell includes a full set of an individual's genes</u> (26).

(2) Do Not Imitate a Source's Syntax and Phrasing

ORIGINAL: If there is a garbage crisis, it is that we are treating garbage as an environmental threat and not what it is: a manageable—though admittedly complex—civic issue. (Poore, Patricia. "America's 'Garbage Crisis.'" *Harper's* Mar. 1994: 39)

PLAGIARISM: If a garbage crisis does exist, it is that people see garbage as a menace to the environment and not what it actually is: a controllable—if obviously complicated—public problem (Poore 39).

Although the preceding passage does not use the exact words of the source, it closely imitates the original's syntax and phrasing, simply substituting synonyms for the author's words.

CORRECT (PARAPHRASE IN WRITER'S OWN WORDS; ONE DISTINCTIVE PHRASE PLACED IN QUOTATION MARKS): Patricia Poore argues that America's "garbage crisis" is exaggerated; rather than viewing garbage as a serious environmental hazard, she says, we should look at garbage as a public problem that may be complicated but that can be solved.

PLAGIARISM AND INTERNET SOURCES

Any time you download text from the Internet, you risk committing plagiarism. To avoid the possibility of plagiarism, do not simply cut and paste blocks of downloaded text directly into your paper. Take the time to summarize or paraphrase this material, copying it into your notes (which may be stored in another file) before you use it in a paper. If you do use the exact words of your source, enclose them in quotation marks and include documentation to identify the source.

(3) Document Statistics Obtained from a Source

Students sometimes assume that statistics are common knowledge. Statistics, however, are usually the result of original research and therefore deserve acknowledgment.

CORRECT: According to one study of 303 accidents recorded, almost one-half took place before the drivers were legally allowed to drive at eighteen (Schuman et al. 1027).

(4) Differentiate Your Words and Ideas from Those of Your Source

ORIGINAL: At some colleges and universities traditional survey courses of world and English literature . . . have been scrapped or diluted. . . . What replaces them is sometimes a mere option of electives, sometimes "multicultural" courses introducing material from Third World cultures and thinning out an already thin sampling of Western writings, and sometimes courses geared especially to issues of class, race, and gender. (Howe, Irving. "The Value of the Canon." *The New Republic* 2 Feb. 1991: 40–47).

PLAGIARISM: At many universities the Western literature survey courses have been edged out by courses that emphasize minority concerns. These courses are "thinning out an already thin sampling of Western writings" in favor of courses geared especially to issues of "class, race, and gender" (Howe 40).

Here it appears that only the quotation in the last sentence is borrowed when, in fact, the first sentence of the passage also owes a debt to the original. A running acknowledgment should come *before* the borrowed material to mark where it begins.

CORRECT: According to critic Irving Howe, at many universities the Western literature survey courses have been edged out by courses that emphasize minority concerns (41). These courses, says Howe, are "thinning out an already thin sampling of Western writings" in favor of "courses geared especially to issues of class, race, and gender" (40).

PART 7

DOCUMENTING SOURCES

CHAPTER 29

MLA DOCUMENTATION FORMAT

Documentation is the formal acknowledgment of the sources you use in your paper. Different academic disciplines use different documentation styles. This chapter explains and illustrates the documentation format recommended by the Modern Language Association (MLA). Chapter 30 discusses the documentation formats of the American Psychological Association (APA), *The Chicago Manual of Style* (*CMS*), and the Council of Biology Editors (CBE).

29a Using MLA Format

MLA format* is required by many teachers of English and other languages as well as teachers in other humanities disciplines. MLA documentation has three parts: *parenthetical references in the text, a list of works cited,* and *content notes.*

(1) Parenthetical References in the Text

MLA documentation uses parenthetical references within the text keyed to a Works Cited list at the end of the paper. A typical reference consists of the author's last name and a page number.

The colony appealed to many idealists in Europe (Ripley 132).

To distinguish two or more sources by the same author, include an appropriate shortened title after the author's name.

Penn emphasized his religious motivation (Kelley, <u>Colonial Years</u> 116).

If you state the author's name or the title of the work in your sentence, do not include it in the parenthetical reference that follows.

Penn's political motivation is discussed by Joseph P. Kelley in <u>Pennsylvania, The Colonial Years, 1681–1776</u> (44).

A period or other punctuation mark follows the parenthetical reference except when a quoted **long prose passage** is set off from the text, in which case the parenthetical reference appears *after* the final punctuation.

See
19a

*MLA documentation format follows the guidelines set in the *MLA Handbook for Writers of Research Papers,* 4th ed. New York, MLA, 1995 with updates from the *MLA Style Manual and Guide to Scholarly Publishing,* 2nd ed. New York, MLA, 1998.

DIRECTORY OF MLA IN-TEXT CITATIONS

1. A work by a single author
2. A work by two or three authors
3. A work by more than three authors
4. A work in multiple volumes
5. A work without a listed author
6. A one-page article
7. An indirect source
8. More than one work
9. A literary work
10. An entire work
11. Two or more authors with the same last name
12. A government document or a corporate author

Sample MLA Parenthetical References

1. A Work by a Single Author
Fairy tales reflect the fears of children (Bettelheim 23).

2. A Work by Two or Three Authors
The historian's main job is to search for clues and solve mysteries (Davidson and Lytle 6).

With the advent of behaviorism, psychology began a new phase of inquiry (Cowen, Barbo, and Crum 31–34).

3. A Work by More than Three Authors
The European powers believed they could change the fundamentals of Moslem existence (Bull et al. 395).

4. A Work in Multiple Volumes If you list more than one volume of a multivolume work in your Works Cited list, include the appropriate volume number.

The French Revolution had a great influence on William Blake (Raine 1:52).

5. A Work without a Listed Author Use a shortened version of the title, beginning with the word by which it is alphabetized in the Works Cited list.

In spite of political unrest Soviet television remained fairly conservative ("Soviet").

6. A One-Page Article Do not include a page reference for a one-page article.

Sixty percent of Arab-Americans work in white-collar jobs (El-Badru).

7. An Indirect Source If you use a statement by one author that is quoted in the work of another author, indicate this with the abbreviation *qtd. in.*

Wagner stated that myth and history stood before him "with opposing claims" (qtd. in Thomas 65).

8. More than One Work

The Brooklyn Bridge has been used as a subject by many American artists (McCullough 144; Tashjian 58).

9. A Literary Work
In a parenthetical reference to a prose work, follow the page number with a semicolon and then add any additional information that may be helpful.

In <u>Moby-Dick</u> Melville refers to a whaling expedition funded by Louis XIV of France (151; ch. 24).

In parenthetical references to long poems, cite both division and line numbers, separating them with a period.

In the <u>Aeneid</u> Virgil describes the ships as cleaving the "green woods reflected in the calm water" (8.124).

In citing classic verse plays, include the act, scene, and line numbers, separated by periods (*Macbeth* 2.2.14–16). In biblical citations include title, chapter, and verse (Genesis 5.12).

10. An Entire Work
When citing an entire work, include the author's name and the work's title in the text.

Herbert Gans's <u>The Urban Villagers</u> is a study of an Italian-American neighborhood in Boston.

11. Two or More Authors with the Same Last Name
To distinguish authors with the same last name, include a first initial.

Recent increases in crime have probably caused thousands of urban homeowners to install burglar alarms (Weishoff, R. 115).

12. A Government Document or a Corporate Author
Cite the organization's name followed by the page number (American Automobile Association 34) or work the organization's name into the text.

According to the President's Commission for the Study of Ethical Problems in Medicine and Biomedical and Behavioral Research, the issues relating to euthanasia are complicated (76).

(2) Works Cited List

The **Works Cited list,** which appears at the end of your paper, gives publication information for all the research materials you cite. If your instructor tells you to list all the sources you read, whether you actually cited them or not, give this list the title *Works Consulted.*

✔ CHECKLIST: PREPARING THE MLA WORKS CITED LIST

See
29a3

✔ Begin the list of works cited on a new page after the last page of text or **content notes**, numbered as the next page of the paper.

✔ Separate the major divisions of each entry—author, title, and publication information—with a period and one space.

✔ List entries alphabetically according to the author's last name. List the author's full name as it appears on the title page of the source. Alphabetize unsigned sources by the first main word of the title.

✔ Do not indent the first line of each entry; indent subsequent lines five spaces (or one-half inch).

✔ Double-space within and between entries.

DIRECTORY OF MLA WORKS CITED ENTRIES

Citations for Books

1. A book by one author
2. A book by two or three authors
3. A book by more than three authors
4. Two or more books by the same author
5. An edited book
6. A selection in an anthology
7. More than one essay from the same anthology
8. A multivolume work
9. The foreword, preface, or afterword of a book
10. A selection in a collection of an author's work
11. A book with a normally underlined title within its title
12. A translation
13. A reprint of an older edition
14. A dissertation (published/unpublished)
15. An article in a reference book (signed/unsigned)
16. A pamphlet
17. A government publication

Citations for Articles

18. An article in a journal with continuous pagination through an annual volume
19. An article in a journal with separate pagination in each issue
20. An article in a weekly magazine (signed/unsigned)
21. An article in a monthly magazine
22. An article that does not appear on consecutive pages

Sample MLA Works Cited Entries: Books Book citations include the author's name, book title (underlined), and publication information (place, publisher, date). Use a short form of the publisher's name (*Alfred A. Knopf, Inc.*, for example, is shortened to *Knopf*, and *Oxford University Press* becomes *Oxford UP*).

1. A Book by One Author
Bettelheim, Bruno. <u>The Uses of Enchantment: The Meaning and Importance of Fairy Tales</u>. New York: Knopf, 1976.

Indicate an edition other than the first as follows.

Gans, Herbert J. <u>The Urban Villagers</u>. 2nd ed. New York: Free, 1982.

2. A Book by Two or Three Authors
Davidson, James West, and Mark Hamilton Lytle. <u>After the Fact: The Art of Historical Detection</u>. New York: Knopf, 1982.

3. A Book by More than Three Authors
Bull, H., et al. <u>The Near East</u>. New York: Oxford UP, 1990.

4. Two or More Books by the Same Author List books by the same author alphabetically by title. After the first entry, use three unspaced hyphens, followed by a period, in place of the author's name.

Thomas, Lewis. <u>The Lives of a Cell: Notes of a Biology Watcher</u>. New York: Viking, 1974.

---. <u>The Medusa and the Snail: More Notes of a Biology Watcher</u>. New York: Viking, 1979.

List such entries alphabetically by title.

5. An Edited Book If your emphasis is on the author's work, begin your citation with the author's name and include the name of the editor after the title.

Bartram, William. <u>The Travels of William Bartram</u>. Ed. Mark Van Doren. New York: Dover, 1955.

If your emphasis is on the editor's work, begin your citation with the editor's name.

Van Doren, Mark, ed. <u>The Travels of William Bartram</u>. By William Bartram. New York: Dover, 1955.

6. A Selection in an Anthology

Lloyd, G. E. R. "Science and Mathematics." <u>The Legacy of Greece</u>. Ed. Moses I. Finley. New York: Oxford UP, 1981. 256–300.

Chopin, Kate. "The Storm." <u>Literature: Reading, Reacting, Writing</u>. Ed. Laurie G. Kirszner and Stephen R. Mandell. Compact 4th ed. Fort Worth: Harcourt, 2000. 138–42.

7. More Than One Essay from the Same Anthology

Bolgar, Robert R. "The Greek Legacy." Finley 429–72.

Finley, Moses I., ed. <u>The Legacy of Greece</u>. New York: Oxford UP, 1981.

Williams, Bernard. "Philosophy." Finley 202–55.

8. A Multivolume Work

Raine, Kathleen. <u>Blake and Tradition</u>. Vol. 1. Princeton: Princeton UP, 1968.

When you use two or more volumes, cite the entire work.

Raine, Kathleen. <u>Blake and Tradition</u>. 2 vols. Princeton: Princeton UP, 1968.

If the volume you are using has an individual title, you may cite the title without mentioning any other volumes. If you wish, however, you may include supplemental information.

Durant, Will, and Ariel Durant. <u>The Age of Napoleon</u>. New York: Simon, 1975. Vol. 11 of <u>The Story of Civilization</u>. 11 vols. 1935–75.

9. The Foreword, Preface, or Afterword of a Book

Taylor, Telford. Preface. <u>Less than Slaves</u>. By Benjamin B. Ferencz.
Cambridge: Harvard UP, 1979. xiii–xxii.

10. A Selection in a Collection of an Author's Work

Walcott, Derek. "Nearing La Guaira." <u>Selected Poems</u>. New York:
Farrar, 1964. 47–48.

11. A Book with a Normally Underlined Title within Its Title

Knoll, Robert E., ed. <u>Storm Over</u> The Waste Land. Chicago: Scott,
1964.

12. A Translation

García Márquez, Gabriel. <u>One Hundred Years of Solitude</u>. Trans.
Gregory Rabassa. New York: Avon, 1991.

13. A Reprint of an Older Edition

Wharton, Edith. <u>The House of Mirth</u>. 1905. New York: Scribner's,
1975.

14. A Dissertation (Published/Unpublished)   For disserta-
tions published by University Microfilms International (UMI),
include the order number.

Peterson, Shawn. <u>Loving Mothers and Lost Daughters: Images of
Female Kinship Relations in Selected Novels of Toni Morrison</u>.
Diss. U of Oregon, 1993. Ann Arbor: UMI, 1994. 9322935.

Use quotation marks for the title of an unpublished dissertation.

Romero, Yolanda Garcia. "The American Frontier Experience in
Twentieth-Century Northwest Texas." Diss. Texas Tech U, 1993.

15. An Article in a Reference Book (Signed/Unsigned)

Drabble, Margaret. "Expressionism." <u>The Oxford Companion to
English Literature</u>. 5th ed. New York: Oxford UP, 1985.

When citing familiar encyclopedias, do not include publication information.

"Cubism." <u>The New Encyclopaedia Britannica: Micropaedia</u>. 1991.

16. A Pamphlet

<u>Existing Light Photography</u>. Rochester: Kodak, 1989.

17. A Government Publication   If the publication has no
listed author, begin with the name of the government, followed
by the name of the agency.

United States. Office of Consumer Affairs. <u>1997 Consumer's Resource
Handbook</u>. Washington: GPO, 1997.

Sample MLA Works Cited Entries: Articles   Article citations
include the author's name, the title of the article (in quotation

marks), the underlined name of the periodical, the date, and page numbers. Month names are abbreviated except for May, June, and July.

18. An Article in a Journal with Continuous Pagination through an Annual Volume

Huntington, John. "Science Fiction and the Future." <u>College English</u> 37 (1975): 340–58.

19. An Article in a Journal with Separate Pagination in Each Issue

Sipes, R. G. "War, Sports, and Aggression: An Empirical Test of Two Rival Theories." <u>American Anthropologist</u> 4.2 (1973): 65–84.

20. An Article in a Weekly Magazine (Signed/Unsigned)

Traub, James. "The Hearts and Minds of City College." <u>New Yorker</u> 7 June 1993: 42–53.

"Solzhenitsyn: A Candle in the Wind." <u>Time</u> 23 Mar. 1970: 70.

21. An Article in a Monthly Magazine

Roll, Lori. "Careers in Engineering." <u>Working Woman</u> Nov. 1982: 62.

22. An Article That Does Not Appear on Consecutive Pages

Griska, Linda. "Stress and Job Performance." <u>Psychology Today</u> Nov.-Dec. 1995: 120+.

23. An Article in a Newspaper (Signed/Unsigned)

Oates, Joyce Carol. "When Characters from the Page Are Made Flesh on the Screen." <u>New York Times</u> 23 Mar. 1986, late ed.: C1+.

"Soviet Television." <u>Los Angeles Times</u> 13 Dec. 1990, sec. 2: 3+.

24. An Editorial

"Tough Cops, Not Brutal Cops." Editorial. <u>New York Times</u> 5 May 1994, late ed.: A26.

25. A Letter to the Editor

Bishop, Jennifer. Letter. <u>Philadelphia Inquirer</u> 10 Dec. 1995: A17.

26. A Book Review

Fox-Genovese, Elizabeth. "Big Mess on Campus." Rev. of <u>Illiberal Education: The Politics of Race and Sex on Campus</u>, by Dinesh D'Souza. <u>Washington Post</u> 15 Apr. 1991, ntnl. weekly ed.: 32.

Sample MLA Works Cited Entries: Nonprint Sources

27. A Lecture

Sandman, Peter. "Communicating Scientific Information." Communications Seminar, Dept. of Humanities and Communications. Drexel U, 26 Oct. 1994.

28. A Personal Interview

West, Cornel. Personal interview. 28 Dec. 1993.

Tannen, Deborah. Telephone interview. 8 June 1994.

29. A Published Interview
Stavros, George. "An Interview with Gwendolyn Brooks."
Contemporary Literature 11.1 (Winter 1970): 1–20.

30. A Personal Letter
Tan, Amy. Letter to the author. 7 Apr. 1990.

31. A Published Letter
Joyce, James. "Letter to Louis Gillet." 20 Aug. 1931. James Joyce. By
Richard Ellmann. New York: Oxford UP, 1965. 631.

32. A Letter in a Library's Archives
Stieglitz, Alfred. Letter to Paul Rosenberg. 5 Sept. 1923. Stieglitz
Archive. Yale, New Haven.

33. A Film
Citizen Kane. Dir. Orson Welles. Perf. Orson Welles, Joseph Cotten,
Dorothy Comingore, and Agnes Moorehead. RKO, 1941.

If you are focusing on the contribution of a particular person, begin with that person's name.

Welles, Orson, dir. Citizen Kane. . . .

34. A Videotape
Interview with Arthur Miller. Dir. William Schiff. Videocassette. The
Mosaic Group, 1987.

35. A Radio or Television Program
"Prime Suspect 3." Writ. Lynda La Plante. Perf. Helen Mirren. Mystery!
WNET, New York. 28 Apr. 1994.

36. A Recording
Boubill, Alain, and Claude-Michel Schönberg. Miss Saigon. Perf. Lea
Salonga, Claire Moore, and Jonathan Pryce. Cond. Martin Koch.
Geffen, 1989.

Marley, Bob. "Crisis." Lyrics. Bob Marley and the Wailers. Kava Island
Records, 1978.

Sample MLA Works Cited Entries: CD-ROMs and Other Portable Databases

37. CD-ROM: Article from a Source with a Print Version
Ingrassia, Michele, and Karen Springen. "She's Not Baby Jessica
Anymore." Newsweek 21 Mar. 1994: 60–65. Infotrac Magazine
Index Plus. CD-ROM. Information Access. Aug. 1995.

38. CD-ROM: Material with no Print Version
"Psychology." Encarta 1996. CD-ROM. Redmond: Microsoft, 1996.

A Music Lover's Multimedia Guide to Beethoven's 5th. CD-ROM.
Spring Valley: Interactive, 1993.

The first of these citations refers to an article from a CD-ROM;
the second, to an entire CD-ROM.

39. A Software Program

Reunion: The Family Tree Software. Vers. 2.0. Diskette. Lester
    Productions, 1994.

Sample MLA Works Cited Entries: Online Databases

40. Article from an Online Source with a Print Version

Weiser, Jay. "The Tyranny of Informality." New Republic 26 Feb. 1996.
    1 Mar. 1996 <http://www.enews.com/magazines/tnr/current/
    022696.3.html>.

The date of the posting was February 26, 1996; the article was
accessed March 1, 1996.

Lacayo, Richard. "Long Distance Calling." Time 17 July 1995: 7 pars.
    20 Nov. 1995. CompuServe.

This article was accessed from the CompuServe computer service. Note that an article accessed through a computer service
does not have an electronic address.

41. Article from an Online Source with No Print Version

"Psychology." Compton's Encyclopedia. Jan. 1996. 6 Jan. 1996.
    America Online.

This entry shows that the material was posted in January 1996
and accessed on January 6, 1996.

42. Electronic Newsletter

"Unprecedented Cutbacks in History of Science Funding." AIP Center
    for History of Physics 27.2 (Fall 1995). 26 Feb. 1996
    <http://www.aip.org/history/fall95.html>.

43. World Wide Web Site

Swofford, Jennifer. The Complete Guide to Keeping Green Iguanas in
    Captivity. 28 July 1995. 5 Mar. 1996 <http://gto.ncsa.uiuc.edu/
    pingleto/herps/iguanacare.html>.

44. E-Mail

Shienvold, Adrianne. "Information on Physical Therapy." E-mail to the
    author. 12 Dec. 1995.

45. Newsgroups

Dudley, Viva. "Is Catnip Safe to Eat?" Online posting. 4 Feb. 1996.
    17 Feb. 1996. <newsalt.animals.felines>.

(3) Content Notes

Content notes—multiple bibliographical citations or other
material (for example, explanations or definitions) that does
not fit smoothly into the text—are indicated by a superscript
(raised numeral) in the paper. Notes can appear either as footnotes at the bottom of the page or as endnotes on a separate
sheet titled *Notes*, placed after the last page of the paper and

before the Works Cited list. Content notes are double-spaced within and between entries.

For Multiple Citations

In the Paper

Many researchers emphasize the necessity of having dying patients share their experiences.[1]

In the Note

[1]Kübler-Ross 27; Stinnette 43; Poston 70; Cohen and Cohen 31–34; Burke 1:91–95.

For Other Material

In the Paper

The massacre during World War I is an event the survivors could not easily forget.[2]

In the Note

[2]For a firsthand account of these events, see Bedoukian 178–81.

29b Sample MLA Manuscript Format

Following are examples of various elements of a research paper that follows MLA format: a title page, an excerpt from a formal outline, two sample pages of the paper, and a Works Cited list.

MLA TITLE PAGE

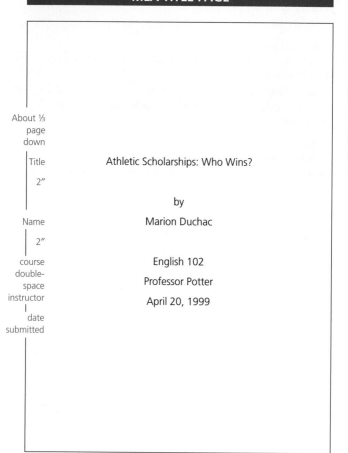

About ⅓ page down

Title — Athletic Scholarships: Who Wins?

2″

by

Name — Marion Duchac

2″

course
double-
space
instructor
|
date
submitted

English 102

Professor Potter

April 20, 1999

MLA 29b

MLA FORMAL OUTLINE

1″   Duchac i

Outline   center

double-
space

<u>Thesis statement:</u> Athletic scholarships should be retained, but college athletic programs should be revamped to deemphasize winning at all costs and to ensure that all student athletes are treated fairly.

I. College athletic programs are valuable.

    A. Athletic programs increase school spirit.

    B. Athletic programs help raise money.

1″

    C. Athletic programs help provide a balanced education.

    D. Athletic scholarships enable disadvantaged students to attend college.

II. Despite their advantages, college athletic programs have problems.

    A. Not all athletes are valued equally.

        1. On many campuses money, equipment, and facilities have been allotted to football and basketball.

        2. Men's sports have been given a disproportionate amount of support.

MLA RESEARCH PAPER SAMPLE PAGE

Duchac 1

Athletic Scholarships: Who Wins?

Athletic scholarships are designed to support physically gifted and talented students. This simple description makes it difficult to envision the problems associated with athletic scholarships, but recently, athletic scholarships and the programs linked with them have become quite controversial. In spite of this controversy, athletic scholarships should be retained, but college athletic programs should be revamped to deemphasize winning at all costs and to ensure that all student athletes are treated fairly.

College athletic programs are certainly valuable. These programs increase school spirit and help to create a sense of community. They also help to raise money: winning teams spark alumni contributions, and athletic events raise funds through ticket sales. In addition, athletic programs--like programs in the performing arts and music--help to provide a rewarding, balanced education for all students. Student athletes make important academic, social, and cultural contributions to their

Thesis statement

1" margin

MLA RESEARCH PAPER SAMPLE PAGE

Duchac 2

schools and thus enrich the college experience for others. Finally, without athletic scholarships, many students would not be able to attend college because, as Alvin Sanoff observes, the aid for which many economically deprived student athletes are eligible does not cover the expense of a college education the way athletic scholarships do (68).

Despite their obvious advantages, college athletic programs have problems. First, not all athletes--or all programs--are valued equally. On many campuses, money, equipment, and facilities have traditionally been allotted to football and basketball at the expense of less visible sports such as swimming, tennis, and field hockey. Men's sports have been given a disproportionate amount of support, and "winning" teams and coaches have been compensated accordingly. In fact, according to Sue M. Durrant, until recently it was not unusual for women's teams to use "hand-me-down" gear while men's teams played with new "state of the art" equipment or for women's teams to travel by bus while men's teams traveled by plane (60).

Material from source, introduced with author's name, ends with parenthetical documentation.

Combination of paraphrase and quotation from a source

MLA WORKS CITED LIST

Works Cited

Works
Cited
page is
numbered
consecu-
tively.

double-
space

Blum, Debra E. "Graduation Rate of Scholarship Athletes
        Rose after Proposition 48 Was Adopted, NCAA
        Reports." <u>Chronicle of Higher Education</u> 7 July
        1993: A42–44.

center

Citation
for signed
newspa-
per article
includes
section
and page
number.

indent five
spaces (or
one-half
inch)

---. "More Freshmen Meet Academic Standards Set by
        NCAA." <u>Chronicle of Higher Education</u> 21 Apr.
        1993: A38–40.

Book by
single
author

Dealy, Francis X. <u>Win at Any Cost</u>. New York: Carol, 1980.

Durrant, Sue M. "Title IX—Its Power and Its Limitations."
        <u>Journal of Physical Education, Recreation and
        Dance</u> 45 (1992): 60–64.

Journal
article

Book by
three
authors

Fleisher, Arthur A., Brian L. Goff, and Robert D. Tollison.
        <u>The National Collegiate Athletic Association</u>.
        Chicago: U of Chicago P, 1992.

Lederman, Douglas. "Men Get 70 Percent of Money
        Available for Athletic Scholarships and Colleges
        That Play Big-Time Sports, New Study Finds."
        <u>Chronicle of Higher Education</u> 18 Mar. 1992: A1+.

MLA WORKS CITED LIST

---. "Men Outnumber Women and Get Most of Money in Big-Time Sports Programs." <u>Chronicle of Higher Education</u> 8 Apr. 1992: A1+.

---. "NCAA Votes Higher Academic Standards for College Athletes." <u>Chronicle of Higher Education</u> 15 Jan. 1992: A1+.

Sanoff, Alvin P. "When Is the Playing Field Too Level?" <u>US News & World Report</u> 30 Jan. 1989: n. pag. Online. CompuServe. 3 Mar. 1994.

Walker, Skippy "Tiptoe." E-mail to the author. 1 Mar. 1996.

"You C.A.N. Get Help with a Scholarship." <u>Scholastic Coach</u> Aug. 1992: 56.

Lederman's name is not repeated in subsequent entries. Three unspaced hyphens are used, followed by a period.

Electronic communication

Unsigned article alphabetized by title

CHAPTER 30

APA AND OTHER DOCUMENTATION FORMATS

 Using APA Format

APA format,* which is used extensively in the social sciences, relies on short parenthetical citations, consisting of the last name of the author, the year of publication, and—for direct quotations—the page number. These references are keyed to an alphabetical list of references that follows the paper. APA format also permits content notes placed after the last page of the text.

(1) Parenthetical References in the Text

When introducing a quotation, include the author's name and the date in the introductory phrase. Put the page number in parentheses after the quotation.

According to Weston (1996), children from one-parent homes read at "a significantly lower level than those from two-parent homes" (p. 58).

When introducing a paraphrase or summary, include the author's name and the date either in the introductory phrase or in parentheses at the end of the paraphrase or summary.

According to Zinn (1995), this program has had success in training teenage fathers to take financial and emotional responsibility for their offspring.

This program has had success in training teenage fathers to take financial and emotional responsibility for their offspring (Zinn, 1995).

Long quotations (forty words or more) are double-spaced and indented five spaces from the left margin. Parenthetical documentation is placed after the final punctuation.

DIRECTORY OF APA IN-TEXT CITATIONS

1. A work by two authors
2. A work by three to five authors
3. A work by six or more authors

*APA documentation format follows the guidelines set in the *Publication Manual of the American Psychological Association,* 4th ed. Washington, DC: APA.

4. A work by a corporate author
5. A work with no listed author
6. A personal communication
7. An indirect source
8. A specific part of a source
9. Two or more works within the same parenthetical reference
10. A table

Sample APA In-Text Citations

1. A Work by Two Authors
There is growing concern over the use of psychological testing in elementary schools (Albright & Glennon, 1982).

2. A Work by Three to Five Authors If a work has more than two but fewer than six authors, mention all names in the first reference, and in subsequent references cite the first author followed by *et al.* and the year.

(Sparks et al., 1984).

3. A Work by Six or More Authors When a work has six or more authors, cite the name of the first author followed by *et al.* and the year in all references.

(Miller et al., 1995).

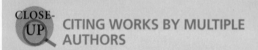

CLOSE-UP CITING WORKS BY MULTIPLE AUTHORS

When referring to multiple authors in the text of your paper, join the last two names with *and*.

According to Rosen, Wolfe, and Ziff (1988). . . .

In parenthetical documentation, however, use an ampersand.

(Rosen, Wolfe, & Ziff, 1988).

4. A Work by a Corporate Author If the name of a corporate author is long, abbreviate it after the first citation.
    First Reference
(National Institute of Mental Health [NIMH], 1994)
    Subsequent Reference
(NIMH, 1994)

5. A Work with No Listed Author   If a work has no listed author, cite the first two or three words of the title (capitalized) and the year.

("New Immigration," 1994).

6. A Personal Communication
(R. Takaki, personal communication, October 17, 1996).

NOTE: Cite letters, memos, telephone conversations, personal interviews, E-mail, messages from electronic bulletin boards, and the like only in the text—*not* in the reference list.

7. An Indirect Source
Cogan and Howe offer very different interpretations of the problem (as cited in Swenson, 1990).

8. A Specific Part of a Source   Use abbreviations for the words *page* (p.), *chapter* (chap.), and *section* (sec.).

These theories have an interesting history (Lee, 1966, chap. 2).

9. Two or More Works within the Same Parenthetical Reference
List works by different authors in alphabetical order.

This theory is supported by several studies (Barson & Roth, 1985; Rose, 1987; Tedesco, 1982).

List works by the same author or authors in order of date of publication.

This theory is supported by several studies (Weiss & Elliot, 1982, 1984, 1985).

For works by the same author published in the same year, designate the work whose title comes first alphabetically *a*, the one whose title comes next *b*, and so on; repeat the year in each citation.

This theory is supported by several studies (Hossack, 1985a, 1985b).

10. A Table   If you use a table from a source, give credit to the author in a note at the bottom of the table.

Note. From "Predictors of Employment and Earnings Among JOBS Participants," P. A. Neenan and D. K. Orthner, 1996, Social Work Research, 20(4), p. 233.

(2) Reference List

The list of all the sources cited in your paper falls at the end on a new numbered page headed *References* (or *Bibliography* if you are listing all the works you consulted, whether or not you cited them).

✓ CHECKLIST: PREPARING THE APA REFERENCE LIST

- ✔ Begin the reference list on a new page after the last page of text or content notes, numbered as the next page of the paper.
- ✔ List the items on the reference list alphabetically (with author's last name first).
- ✔ Indent the first line of each entry five to seven spaces; type subsequent lines flush with the left-hand margin. (If your instructor prefers, you may instead type the first line of each entry flush with the left margin and indent subsequent lines three spaces.)
- ✔ Separate the major divisions of each entry with a period and one space.
- ✔ Double-space the reference list within and between entries.

✓ CHECKLIST: ARRANGING WORKS IN THE APA REFERENCE LIST

- ✔ Single-author entries precede multiple-author entries that begin with the same name.

Field, S. (1987).

Field, S., & Levitt, M. P. (1984).

- ✔ Entries by the same author or authors are arranged according to date of publication, starting with the earliest date.

Ruthenberg, H., & Rubin, R. (1985).

Ruthenberg, H., & Rubin, R. (1987).

- ✔ Entries with the same author or authors and date of publication are arranged alphabetically according to title.

Wolk, E. M. (1986a). Analysis . . .

Wolk, E. M. (1986b). Hormonal . . .

DIRECTORY OF APA REFERENCE LIST ENTRIES

Citations for Books
1. A book with one author
2. A book with more than one author

3. An edited book
4. A book with no listed author or editor
5. A work in several volumes
6. A work with a corporate author
7. A government report
8. One selection from an anthology
9. An article in a reference book
10. The foreword, preface, or afterword of a book

Citations for Articles
11. An article in a scholarly journal with continuous pagination through an annual volume
12. An article in a scholarly journal with separate pagination in each issue
13. A magazine article
14. A newspaper article (signed/unsigned)
15. A letter to the editor
16. A published letter

Citations for Electronic Media
17. Online article
18. Abstract on CD-ROM
19. Abstract online
20. Computer software

Sample APA Reference List Entries: Books Capitalize only the first word of the title and subtitle. Underline the entire title, including punctuation, and enclose the date, volume number, and edition number in parentheses. Write out the publisher's name in full.

1. A Book with One Author
    Maslow, A. H. (1974). <u>Toward a psychology of being.</u> Princeton: Van Nostrand.

2. A Book with More Than One Author List all the authors—by last name and initials—regardless of how many there are.

    Wolfinger, D., Knable, P., Richards, H. L., & Silberger, R. (1990). <u>The chronically unemployed.</u> New York: Berman Press.

3. An Edited Book
    Lewin, K., Lippitt, R., & White, R. K. (Eds.). (1985). <u>Social learning and imitation.</u> New York: Basic Books.

4. A Book with No Listed Author or Editor
    <u>Writing with a computer.</u> (1993). Philadelphia: Drexel Publications.

5. A Work in Several Volumes
    Jones, P. R., & Williams, T. C. (Eds.). (1990–1993). <u>Handbook of therapy</u> (Vols. 1–2). Princeton: Princeton University Press.

6. A Work with a Corporate Author
  League of Women Voters of the United States. (1991). <u>Local league handbook.</u> Washington, DC: Author.

NOTE: When the author and publisher are the same, list *Author* at the end of the citation instead of repeating the publisher's name.

7. A Government Report
  National Institute of Mental Health. (1987). <u>Motion pictures and violence: A summary report of research</u> (DHHS Publication No. ADM 91-22187). Washington, DC: U.S. Government Printing Office.

8. One Selection from an Anthology
  Lorde, A. (1984). Age, race, and class. In P. S. Rothenberg (Ed.), <u>Racism and sexism: An integrated study</u> (pp. 352–360). New York: St. Martin's.

NOTE: A title of a selection in an anthology is not underlined or enclosed in quotation marks. If you cite two or more selections from the same anthology, give the full citation in each entry.

9. An Article in a Reference Book
  Edwards, P. (Ed.). (1987). Determinism. In <u>The encyclopedia of philosophy</u> (Vol. 2, pp. 359–373). New York: Macmillan.

10. The Foreword, Preface, or Afterword of a Book
  Taylor, T. (1979). Preface. In <u>Less than slaves</u> by Benjamin B. Ferencz. Cambridge: Harvard University Press.

Sample APA Reference List Entries: Articles Capitalize only the first word of the title and subtitle. Do not underline the title of the article or enclose it in quotation marks. Give the periodical title in full; underline the title and capitalize all major words. Underline the volume number but not the issue number in parentheses. Give inclusive page numbers. Use *pp.* when referring to page numbers in newspapers, but omit this abbreviation when referring to page numbers in periodicals with volume numbers.

11. An Article in a Scholarly Journal with Continuous Pagination through an Annual Volume
  Miller, W. (1969). Violent crimes in city gangs. <u>Journal of Social Issues 27,</u> 581–593.

12. An Article in a Scholarly Journal with Separate Pagination in Each Issue
  Williams, S., & Cohen, L. R. (1984). Child stress in early learning situations. <u>American Psychologist, 21</u> (10), 1–28.

13. A Magazine Article
  McCurdy, H. G. (1983, June). Brain mechanisms and intelligence. <u>Psychology Today,</u> pp. 61–63.

14. A Newspaper Article (Signed/Unsigned)

James, W. R. (1993, November 16). The uninsured and health care. <u>The Wall Street Journal,</u> pp. A1, A14.

Article appears on two separate pages.

Study finds many street people mentally ill. (1993, June 7). <u>New York Times,</u> p. A7.

15. A Letter to the Editor

Williams, P. (1993, July 19). Self-fulfilling stereotypes [Letter to the editor]. <u>Los Angeles Times,</u> p. A22.

16. A Published Letter

Joyce, J. (1931). Letter to Louis Gillet. In Richard Ellmann, <u>James Joyce</u> (p. 631). New York: Oxford University Press.

17. Online Article

Farrell, P. D. (1997, March). New high-tech stresses hit traders and investors on the information superhighway. [14 paragraphs.] <u>Wall Street News</u> [Online serial]. Available http: wall-street-news.com/forecasts/stress/stress.html

NOTE: No period follows the electronic address.

18. Abstract on CD-ROM

Guiot, A., & Peterson, B. R. (1995). Forgetfulness and partial cognition. [CD-ROM]. <u>Memory and Cognition, 23,</u> 643–652. Abstract from: SilverPlatter File: PsycLit Item: 90-14321

19. Abstract Online

Guiot, A., & Peterson, B. R. (1995). Forgetfulness and partial cognition. [Online]. <u>Memory and Cognition, 23,</u> 643–652. Abstract from: DIALOG file: PsycINFO Item: 90-14321

20. Computer Software

Sharp, S. (1995). *Career Selection Tests* (Version 5.0) [Computer software]. Chico, CA: Avocation Software.

(3) Content Notes

APA format allows, but does not encourage, the use of content notes, indicated by **superscripts** (raised numerals) in the text. The notes are listed on a separate numbered page, entitled *Footnotes*, following the last page of text. Double-space all notes, indenting the first line of each note five to seven spaces and beginning subsequent lines flush left.

(4) Sample APA Manuscript Format

Following are examples of various elements of an APA research paper: a title page, two sample pages of the paper, and a reference list.

APA TITLE PAGE

Student Stress 1 — Page header, page number

Type running head flush with left-hand margin — Running head: STUDENT STRESS

Student Stress and Attrition

Gloria E. Medrano

University of Texas at El Paso

Center title, name, and school

APA RESEARCH PAPER SAMPLE PAGE

Student Stress 2

Full title

Student Stress and Attrition

Statistic used in introduction

Ecklund and Henderson (1981), in their national longitudinal study of the high school class of 1972, documented how 46% of enrolling college freshmen had at one point or another dropped out of college. Thirty-four percent dropped out within their first two years (Ecklund & Henderson, 1981). The high dropout rate,

Author's name in parentheses when not mentioned in text

along with a decreasing student population (Dusek & Renteria, 1984), is still directly affecting the state of our educational system today. Although there is little that can be done about the lower numbers of incoming freshmen, something can be done to lessen the problem of college attrition.

Thesis statement

The ideal approach to combatting this problem is to deal with the group of students closest in proximity to the university--the residence hall population. Many of their reasons for withdrawing from the university are traced to a fundamental cause: stress. In this case stress is the

Page header and number on every page

APA RESEARCH PAPER SAMPLE PAGE

Student Stress 3

psychological phenomenon that contributes to the high

attrition rates of resident students.

Statement of the Problem

The on-campus resident student population is very

different from other groups of individuals. They cannot be

compared to such groups as nonstudents, noncommuters,

and commuters. Aside from such student-related stressors

as academics and personal, financial, and emotional

problems, on-campus residents must also contend with

adjusting to their new environment, living away from

home and in a new community, having a roommate, and

being disturbed by the over-all noise level in the

dormitories.

Bishop and Snyder (1976) noted grades and money as

the major pressures that account for the differences between

residents and commuters. Commuters ranked time

management next on their list, and residents listed social

pressures and concerns about their future as their next most

Margin notes:

Identifies and describes the group to be studied, distinguishing it from other groups.

Headings included in the text. See **A3** for format.

Year in parentheses, authors' names in text

APA REFERENCE LIST

Student Stress 6

Center
Double-
space

References

Bishop, J. B., & Snyder, G. S. (1976). Commuters and

residents. Pressures, helps and psychological services.

<u>Journal of College Student Personnel, 17,</u> 232–235.

Indent ⟶   Dusek, R., & Renteria, R. (1984, December 13). Plan
first line
of each   slashes UTEP budget by 28%. <u>El Paso Times,</u> p. A1.
entry five
to seven   Ecklund, B. K., & Henderson, L. B. (1981).
spaces*
<u>Longitudinal study of the high school class of 1972.</u>

Washington, DC: National Institute of Education. (Eric

Document Reproduction Service No. ED 311 222)

Reference
page
numbered
consecu-
tively

Journal
article by
two
authors

News-
paper
article

Document
from
computer
database

---

*This format is now recommended by the APA for all manuscripts sub-
mitted for publication. If your instructor prefers, you may instead type the
first line of each entry flush with the left-hand margin and indent subsequent lines three spaces.

30b Using CMS Format

The Chicago Manual of Style (CMS) is used in history and some social science and humanities disciplines. **CMS format*** has two parts: notes at the end of the paper (endnotes) and a list of bibliographic citations. (Although Chicago style encourages the use of endnotes, it also allows the use of footnotes at the bottom of the page.)

(1) Endnotes and Footnotes

The notes format calls for a **superscript** (raised numeral) in the text after source material you have either quoted or referred to. This numeral, placed after all punctuation marks except dashes, corresponds to the numeral that accompanies the note.

✔ **CHECKLIST: PREPARING THE CMS ENDNOTES**

- ✔ Begin endnotes on a new page after the last page of the paper.
- ✔ Number the page on which the endnotes appear as the next page of the paper.
- ✔ Type and number notes in the order in which they appear in the paper, beginning with number 1.
- ✔ Type the note number on the line, followed by a period and one space.
- ✔ Indent the first line of each note three spaces; type subsequent lines flush with the left-hand margin.
- ✔ Double-space within and between entries.

Endnote and Footnote Format: CMS

In the Text

By November of 1942, the Allies had proof that the Nazis were engaged in the systemic killing of Jews.[1]

In the Note

1. David S. Wyman, *The Abandonment of the Jews: America and the Holocaust 1941–1945* (New York: Pantheon Books, 1984), 65.

(2) Bibliography

In addition to the heading *Bibliography,* Chicago style allows *Selected Bibliography, Works Cited, Literature Cited, References,* and *Sources Consulted.*

---

*The CMS format follows the guidelines set in *The Chicago Manual of Style,* 14th ed. Chicago: University of Chicago Press, 1993.

✔ CHECKLIST: PREPARING THE CMS BIBLIOGRAPHY

- ✔ Type entries on a separate page after the endnotes.
- ✔ List entries alphabetically according to the author's last name.
- ✔ Type the first line of each entry flush with the left-hand margin; indent subsequent lines three spaces.
- ✔ Double-space the bibliography within and between entries.

DIRECTORY OF CMS ENDNOTE AND BIBLIOGRAPHY ENTRIES

Entries for Books

1. A book by one author
2. A book by two or three authors
3. A book by more than three authors
4. An edited book
5. A chapter in a book or an essay in an anthology
6. A multivolume work

Entries for Articles

7. An article in a scholarly journal with continuous pagination through an annual volume
8. An article in a scholarly journal with separate pagination in each issue
9. An article in a weekly magazine
10. An article in a monthly magazine
11. An article in a newspaper

Entries for Nonprint Sources

12. A personal interview
13. A published interview
14. A letter
15. A film or videotape
16. A recording

Entries for Electronic Sources

17. Computer software
18. An electronic document

Subsequent References

Sample Chicago Manual of Style Endnote and Bibliography Entries Although underlining to indicate italics is acceptable, Chicago style recommends the use of italics for titles.

Sample CMS Entries: Books

1. A Book by One Author
Endnote
1. Herbert J. Gans, *The Urban Villagers,* 2d ed. (New York: Free Press, 1982), 100.
Bibliography
Gans, Herbert J. *The Urban Villagers,* 2d ed. New York: Free Press, 1982.

2. A Book by Two or Three Authors
Endnote
2. James W. Davidson and Mark Hamilton Lytle, *After the Fact: The Art of Historical Detection* (New York: Alfred A. Knopf, 1982), 54.
Bibliography
Davidson, James W., and Mark Hamilton Lytle. *After the Fact: The Art of Historical Detection.* New York: Alfred A. Knopf, 1982.

3. A Book by More than Three Authors
Endnote
3. Robert E. Spiller et al., eds., *Literary History of the United States* (New York: Macmillan, 1974), 24.
Bibliography
Spiller, Robert E., et al., eds. *Literary History of the United States.* New York: Macmillan, 1974.

4. An Edited Book
Endnote
4. William Bartram, *The Travels of William Bartram,* ed. Mark Van Doren (New York: Dover Press, 1955), 85.
Bibliography
Bartam, William. *The Travels of William Bartram.* Edited by Mark Van Doren. New York: Dover Press, 1955.

5. A Chapter in a Book or an Essay in an Anthology
Endnote
5. Peter Kidson, "Architecture and City Planning," in *The Legacy of Greece,* ed. M. I. Finley (New York: Oxford University Press, 1981), 376–400.
Bibliography
Kidson, Peter. "Architecture and City Planning." In *The Legacy of Greece,* ed. M. I. Finley, 376–400. New York: Oxford University Press, 1981.

6. A Multivolume Work
Endnote
6. Kathleen Raine, *Blake and Tradition* (Princeton: Princeton University Press, 1968), 1: 143.
Bibliography
Raine, Kathleen. *Blake and Tradition.* Vol. 1. Princeton: Princeton University Press, 1968.

Sample CMS Entries: Articles

   7. An Article in a Scholarly Journal with Continuous Pagination through an Annual Volume
Endnote
7. John Huntington, "Science Fiction and the Future," *College English* 37 (fall 1975): 341.
Bibliography
Huntington, John. "Science Fiction and the Future." *College English* 37 (fall 1975): 340–58.

   8. An Article in a Scholarly Journal with Separate Pagination in Each Issue
Endnote
8. R. G. Sipes, "War, Sports, and Aggression: An Empirical Test of Two Rival Theories," *American Anthropologist* 4, no. 2 (1973): 80.
Bibliography
Sipes, R. G. "War, Sports, and Aggression: An Empirical Test of Two Rival Theories." *American Anthropologist* 4, no. 2 (1973): 65–84.

   9. An Article in a Weekly Magazine
Endnote
9. James Traub, "The Hearts and Minds of City College," *New Yorker,* 7 June 1993, 45.
Bibliography
Traub, James. "The Hearts and Minds of City College." *New Yorker,* 7 June 1993, 42–53.

   10. An Article in a Monthly Magazine
Endnote
10. Lori Roll, "Careers in Engineering," *Working Woman,* November 1982, 62.
Bibliography
Roll, Lori. "Careers in Engineering." *Working Woman,* November 1982, 62.

   11. An Article in a Newspaper
Endnote
11. Raymond Bonner, "A Guatemalan General's Rise to Power," *New York Times,* 21 July 1982, 3(A).
Bibliography
Bonner, Raymond. "A Guatemalan General's Rise to Power." *New York Times,* 21 July 1982, 3(A).

Sample CMS Entries: Nonprint Sources

   12. A Personal Interview
Endnote
12. Cornel West, interview by author, tape recording, St. Louis, Mo., 8 June 1994.
Bibliography
West, Cornel. Interview by author. Tape recording. St. Louis, Mo., 8 June 1994.

13. A Published Interview

Endnote

13. Gwendolyn Brooks, interview by George Stravos, *Contemporary Literature* 11, no. 1 (winter 1970): 12.

Bibliography

Brooks, Gwendolyn. Interview by George Stravos. *Contemporary Literature* 11, no. 1 (winter 1970): 1–20.

14. A Letter

Endnote

14. Amy Tan, letter to author, 7 April 1990.

Bibliography

Tan, Amy. Letter to author. 7 April 1990.

15. A Film or Videotape

Endnote

15. *Interview with Arthur Miller,* dir. William Schiff, 17 min., The Mosaic Group, 1987, videocassette.

Bibliography

Miller, Arthur. *Interview with Arthur Miller.* Directed by William Schiff. 17 min. The Mosaic Group, 1987. Videocassette.

16. A Recording

Endnote

16. Bob Marley, "Crisis," on *Bob Marley and the Wailers,* Kava Island Records compact disk 423 095-3.

Bibliography

Marley, Bob. "Crisis." On *Bob Marley and the Wailers.* Kava Island Records compact disk 423 095-3.

Sample CMS Entries: Electronic Sources

17. Computer Software

Endnote

17. *Reunion: The Family Tree Software,* vers. 2.0 for Macintosh, Lester Productions, Cambridge, Mass.

Bibliography

Reunion: The Family Tree Software. Vers. 2.0 for Macintosh. Lester Productions, Cambridge, Mass.

18. An Electronic Document *The Chicago Manual of Style* recommends following the guidelines developed by the International Standards Organization (ISO). List the authors, the title, the electronic medium (electronic bulletin board, for example), information about a print version, access dates, and electronic address or location information.

Endnote

18. Arthur Sklar, "Survey of Legal Opinions Regarding the Death Penalty in New Jersey," in NL-KR (Digest vol. 3, no. 2) [electronic bulletin board] (Newark, N.J., 1995 [cited 17 March 1997]); available from nl-kr@cs.newark.edu; INTERNET.

APA and Other Formats

Bibliography

Sklar, Arthur. "Survey of Legal Opinions Regarding the Death Penalty in New Jersey," in NL-KR (Digest vol. 3, no. 2) [electronic bulletin board]. (Newark, N.J., 1995 [cited 17 March 1997]. Available from nl-kr@cs.newark.edu; INTERNET.

Sample CMS Entries: Subsequent References   In the first reference to a work, use the full citation; in subsequent references to the same work, list only the author's last name, followed by a comma and a page number.

First Note on Espinoza
1. J. M. Espinoza, *The First Expedition of Vargas in New Mexico, 1692* (Albuquerque: University of New Mexico Press, 1949), 10–12.
Subsequent Note
5. Espinoza, 29.

NOTE: *The Chicago Manual of Style* allows the use of the abbreviation *ibid.* ("in the same place") for subsequent references to the same work as long as there are no intervening references. *Ibid.* takes the place of the author's name and the work's title—but not the page number.

First Note on Espinoza
1. J. M. Espinoza, *The First Expedition of Vargas in New Mexico, 1692* (Albuquerque: University of New Mexico Press, 1949), 10–12.
Subsequent Note
2. Ibid., 23.

Keep in mind, however, that the use of *Ibid.* is giving way to the use of the author's last name and the page number for subsequent references to the same work.

30c Using CBE Format

Documentation formats recommended by the Council of Biological Editors (CBE) are used in biology, botany, zoology, physiology, anatomy, and genetics. *The CBE Style Manual* recommends several documentation styles, including the number-reference format described below. This format calls for either raised numbers in the text of the paper (the preferred form) or numbers inserted parenthetically in the text.

One study[1] has demonstrated the effect of low dissolved oxygen.

These numbers correspond to a list titled *References, Literature Cited,* or *References Cited* at the end of the paper.

NOTE: If you refer to more than one source in a single note, the numbers are separated by a dash if they are in sequence ([2-3]) and by a comma if they are not ([3, 6]).

✔ CHECKLIST: PREPARING THE CBE REFERENCE LIST

✔ Begin the reference list on a new page after the last page of the paper, numbered as the next page of the paper.

✔ List the items in the order in which they appear in the paper, not alphabetically.

✔ Number the entries consecutively; type the note numbers on (not above) the line, followed by a period.

✔ Type the first line of each entry flush with the left-hand margin; align subsequent lines directly beneath the first letter of the author's last name.

✔ Double-space within and between entries.

DIRECTORY OF CBE REFERENCE LIST ENTRIES

1. A book with one author
2. A book with more than one author
3. An edited book
4. A specific section of a book
5. A chapter in a book or an essay in an anthology
6. An article in a journal with continuous pagination
7. An article in a journal with separate pagination in each issue
8. An article with no listed author
9. An electronic source

Sample CBE Reference List Entries: Books List the author or authors (last name first), the title (not underlined, and with only the first word capitalized), the place of publication (followed by a colon), the full name of the publisher (followed by a semicolon), the year (followed by a period), and the total number of pages (followed by a period).

1. A Book with One Author

1. Key, K. Plant biology. Fort Worth: Harcourt Brace; 1995. 437 p.

2. A Book with More Than One Author

2. Krause, KF, Paterson, MK. Tissue culture: methods and application. New York: Academic Press; 1993. 217 p.

3. An Edited Book

3. Marzacco, MP, editor. A survey of biochemistry. New York: Bowker; 1985. 523 p.

4. A Specific Section of a Book

4. Baldwin, LD, Rigby, CV. A study of animal virology. New York: Wiley; 1984: p 121–133.

5. A Chapter in a Book or an Essay in an Anthology

5. Brydon, RB, Ellis, J, Scott, CD. Cell division and cancer treatment. In Gotlieb, JM. editor. Current research in cancer treatment. New York: Springer-Verlag; 1996: p. 34–47.

Sample CBE Reference List Entries: Articles List the author or authors (last name first), the title of the article (with only the first word capitalized), the abbreviated name of the journal (with all major words capitalized, but not underlined), the year (followed by a semicolon), the volume number (followed by a colon), and inclusive page numbers. No spaces separate the year, the volume, and the page numbers.

6. An Article in a Journal with Continuous Pagination

6. Bensley, KR. Profiling women physicians. Medica 1985; 1:140–145.

7. An Article in a Journal with Separate Pagination in Each Issue

7. Paul, DR, Wang, AR, Richards, L. The human genome project. Sci Am 1995 Sept;285(2):43–52.

8. An Article with No Listed Author

8. [Anonymous]. Developments in microbiology. Int. J. Microbiol 1987;6:234–248.

9. An Electronic Source List the author or authors, the title (followed by the journal title, along with the date and volume number, in the case of journal articles), the electronic medium [*serial on-line* for periodicals and *monograph on-line* for books], the date of publication, the words *Available from* followed by a colon and the electronic address, and the date of access.

9. Bensley, KR. Profiling women physicians. Medica [serial on-line] 1985;1. Available from: ftp.lib.nscu.edu via the INTERNET. Accessed 1997 Feb 18.

30d Using Other Documentation Styles

The following style manuals describe documentation formats used in other disciplines.

Chemistry

American Chemical Society. *Handbook for Authors of Papers in American Chemical Society Publications.* Washington: American Chemical Soc., 1986.

Geology

United States Geological Survey. *Suggestions to Authors of the Reports of the United States Geological Survey.* 7th ed. Washington: GPO, 1991.

Law

The Bluebook: A Uniform System of Citation. Comp. Editors of
  Columbia Law Review et al. 15th ed. Cambridge: Harvard Law
  Review, 1991.

Linguistics

Linguistic Society of America. "LSA Style Sheet." Published annually in
  December issue of the *LSA Bulletin*.

Mathematics

American Mathematical Society. *A Manual for Authors of
  Mathematical Papers.* Rev. Ed. Providence: AMS, 1990.

Medicine

Iverson, Cheryl, et al. *American Medical Association Manual of Style.*
  8th ed. Baltimore: Williams and Wilkins, 1989.

Music

Holman D. Kirn, ed. *Writing about Music: A Style Sheet from the
  Editors of 19th-Century Music.* Berkeley: U California P, 1988.

Physics

American Institute of Physics. *AIP Style Manual.* 4th ed. New York:
  Am. Inst. of Physics, 1990.

Scientific and Technical Writing

Rubens, Philip, ed. *Science and Technical Writing: A Manual of Style.*
  Fort Worth: Harcourt, 1992.

PART 8

APPENDICES

APPENDIX A

DOCUMENT DESIGN AND FORMAT

Some of your instructors will give you specific guidelines for formatting a paper—and, of course, you should follow them. This chapter presents general guidelines for document design as well as specific manuscript guidelines for the humanities and the social sciences and formats for business letters and résumés.

A1 Document Design

Document design refers to the conventions that determine the way a document—a research paper, memo, report, business letter, or résumé, for example—looks on a page.

Margins Your document should be double-spaced (unless you are told otherwise), with at least a one-inch margin on all sides.

Font Size To create a readable document, use a 10- or 12-point font. Avoid fonts that will distract readers (script or cursive fonts, for example).

White Space You can use white space around a block of text—a paragraph or a section, for example—to focus readers' attention on the material you are isolating.

(1) Using Headings

Headings tell readers what to expect in a section before they actually read it. By breaking up a text, headings make a document seem inviting and easy to read.

Number of Headings The number of headings depends on the document. A long, complicated document will need more headings than a shorter, less complex one. Keep in mind that while too few headings may not be of much use, too many headings will make your document look like an outline.

Phrasing Headings should be brief, descriptive, and to the point. They can be single words—*Summary* or *Introduction*, for example. Headings can also be phrases (always stated in **parallel** terms): *Choosing a dog, Caring for the dog, Housebreaking the dog.* They can also be questions (*How do you choose a dog?*) or statements (*Choose a dog carefully*).

See
12a

Format Headings and subheadings may be *centered*, placed *flush left*, or *indented*. The most important thing to remember is that headings at the same level should have the same format—for example, if one first-level heading is boldfaced and centered, all other first-level headings must be boldfaced and centered.

Typographical Emphasis You can emphasize important words in headings by using **boldface,** *italics,* or ALL CAPITAL LETTERS. Used in moderation, these distinctive typefaces make a text more readable. Used excessively, however, they slow readers down.

NOTE: MLA style recommends that headings be in the same type as the rest of the paper.

(2) Constructing Lists

A list separates material and enables readers to see it easily. A list can also break up complicated statements into a series of key ideas. Lists are easiest to read when all the elements are parallel and about the same length. When rank is important, number the items on the list; when it isn't, use **bullets** (as in the list below). Make sure you introduce the list with a complete sentence followed by a colon.

There are several steps we should take to reduce our spending:
- We should cut our workforce by 10 percent.
- We should utilize less expensive vendors.
- We should decrease overtime.

Because the items on the list above are complete sentences, each ends with a period. Do not use periods if the items are not sentences.

(3) Tables, Graphs, Diagrams, and Photographs

Visuals, such as tables, graphs, diagrams, and photographs, can often be used to enhance your documents. You can create your own tables and graphs by using a computer program like *Excel* or *Lotus.* In addition, you can get diagrams and photographs by photocopying or scanning them from a print source or by downloading them from the Internet or CD-ROM encyclopedias. Remember, however, that if you use a visual from a source, you *must* use appropriate **documentation.**

See
Pt. 7

Tables Tables present data in a condensed, visual format—arranged in rows and columns. Tables most often contain numerical data, although occasionally they contain words as well as numbers. Keep in mind that tables may distract readers, so include only those that are necessary to support your discussion. The following table summarizes personnel data.

McVay 3

As the following table shows, the Madison location now employs more workers in every site than the St. Paul location.

Table 1   Heading

Number of Employees at Each Location   Descriptive
                                                           caption
                        Location

Employees	Madison	St. Paul	
Plant	461	254	Data
Warehouse	45	23	
Outlet Stores	15	9	

Because the Madison location has grown so quickly, steps must be taken to. . . .

Graphs Whereas tables present specific numerical data, graphs convey the general pattern or trend that the data suggest. Because graphs tend to be more general (and therefore less accurate) than tables, they are frequently accompanied by tables. The following is an example of a bar graph.

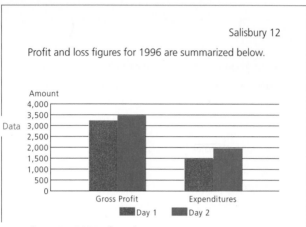

Salisbury 12

Profit and loss figures for 1996 are summarized below.

Label and descriptive caption   Figure 1. 1996 Profit and Loss

Source: Charles Gainor, "Gross Profit and Loss in Government

Citation   Procurement," <u>Defense Department Expenditure Quarterly</u>

(Washington, DC: GPO, 1997) 37.

Clearly, these figures indicate. . . .

Document Design

Diagrams A diagram enables you to focus on specific details of a mechanism or object. Diagrams are often used in scientific and technical writing to clarify concepts while eliminating paragraphs of detailed and confusing description. The diagram below, which illustrates the ancient Greek theater, serves a similar purpose in a literature paper.

Dixon 10

The design of the ancient Greek theater is similar to that of a present-day sports stadium, as figure 2 illustrates.

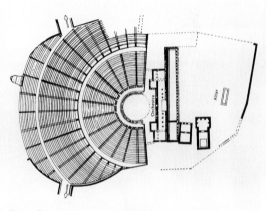

Label Figure 2.

The Theater of Dionysus at Athens. Redrawn from a drawing by R. C. Flickinger, <u>The Greek Theater and Its Drama</u> (1918).

Citation

Descriptive caption

This design, with its tiered seats, enabled the audience to view the actors onstage as well as. . . .

Photographs Photographs enable you to show exactly what something or someone looks like—an animal in its natural habitat, a work of fine art, or an actor in costume, for example. Although computer technology that enables you to paste photographs directly into a text is widely available, you should use it with restraint. Not every photograph will support or enhance your written text; in fact, an irrelevant photograph will distract readers.

Robes 3

In the later years of his life, Twain was seen more as a personality than as a writer. Figure 3 shows him in a characteristic pose.

Label Figure 3.

Descriptive Mark Twain, on porch with kitten.
caption

The white suit he wears in this photograph. . . .

> ✔ **CHECKLIST: INCLUDING VISUALS IN THE TEXT**
>
> ✔ Use a visual only when it contributes something important to the discussion, not for embellishment.
> ✔ Include the visual in the text only if you plan to discuss it in your paper (place the visual in an appendix if you do not).
> ✔ Introduce each visual with a complete sentence.
> ✔ Follow each visual with a discussion of its significance.
> ✔ Leave wide margins around each visual.
> ✔ Place the visual as close as possible to the section of your document in which it is discussed.
> ✔ Label each visual appropriately.
> ✔ Document each visual that is borrowed from a source.

A2 MLA Manuscript Guidelines

MLA guidelines are used for papers in the humanities. The following guidelines are based on the *MLA Handbook for Writers of Research Papers*.

1. Type your paper with a one-inch margin at the top and bottom and on both sides. Double-space your paper throughout.
2. Indent the first line of every paragraph, as well as the first line of every item on the Works Cited list, five spaces (or one-half inch). Set a long prose quotation (more than four lines) off from the text by indenting ten spaces (or one inch).
3. If your instructor does not require a separate title page, use the model on page A-10 for the first page of your paper.
4. If your instructor requires a separate title page, use a format like the one used in the paper in **29b.**
5. Number all pages of your paper consecutively—including the first—in the upper right-hand corner, one-half inch from the top, flush right. Type your name before the page number on every page.
6. If you use source material in your paper, follow **MLA documentation style** See Ch. 29

FIRST PAGE OF MLA PAPER WITHOUT TITLE PAGE

½″
Duchac 1

1″

Marion Duchac
Professor Potter   ← Double-space
English 102
20 April 1994

       Athletic Scholarships: Who Wins?   ← Double-space

     Athletic scholarships are designed to aid physically

1″ → gifted and talented students in the pursuit of education   1″ ←→

and sport. This simple description makes it difficult to

envision the problems associated with athletic

scholarships, but recently, athletic scholarships and the

programs linked with them have become quite

controversial. In spite of this controversy, athletic

scholarships should be retained, but college athletic

programs should be revamped to deemphasize winning

at all costs and to ensure that all student athletes are

treated fairly.

A3   APA Manuscript Guidelines

APA guidelines are used for papers in the social sciences. The following guidelines are based on the *Publication Manual of the American Psychological Association* (4th ed.).

1. Type your paper with at least a one-inch margin at the top, bottom, and sides of the paper. Do not hyphenate words at the end of a line. Double-space between all lines of the manuscript.
2. Indent the first line of every paragraph, as well as the first line of every item on the Reference List, five to seven spaces. Set off quotations of forty or more words in a block format placed five to seven spaces from the left-hand margin.
3. The title page should follow the model on page 155.
4. Papers in the social sciences often contain an **abstract,** a short summary of approximately one hundred words. If your

instructor requires an abstract, it should appear as a separate numbered page (labeled *Abstract*) after the title page.

5. Number all pages of your paper consecutively. Each page should include the running head as well as the page number in the upper right-hand corner.

6. Major **headings** should be centered and typed with upper-case and lowercase letters. Minor headings should be flush left, typed with uppercase and lowercase letters, and underlined. See A1.1

7. Items in a series should be formatted as a numbered **list** See A1.2

8. If you use source material in your paper, citations should be consistent with **APA documentation style** See Ch. 30

A4   Business Letter and Résumé Format

You may write business letters for a variety of reasons—for example, to request information, to complain about a product or service, or to thank someone. One of the most common business letters is a **letter of application,** which summarizes your qualifications for a specific job. This letter is almost always accompanied by a **résumé,** which provides a general overview of your accomplishments. Formats for a letter of application and a résumé appear on the following pages.

SAMPLE LETTER OF APPLICATION—
SEMIBLOCK FORMAT

Heading

246 Hillside Drive
Urbana, IL 61801
October 20, 1999
kr237@metropolis.105.com

Mr. Maurice Snyder, Personnel Director
Guilford, Fox, and Morris
Inside   22 Hamilton Street
address Urbana, IL 61822

Salutation   Dear Mr. Snyder:

My college advisor, Dr. Raymond Walsh, has told me that you
are interested in hiring a part-time accounting assistant. I believe
that my academic background and my work experience qualify
me for this position.

Body   I am presently a junior accounting major at the University of
Illinois. During the past year, I have taken courses in taxation,
trusts, and business law. I am also proficient in *Lotus* and
ClarisWorks. Last spring, I gained practical accounting
experience by working in our department's tax clinic.

Double- ⟶
space   After I graduate, I hope to get a master's degree in taxation and
          then return to the Urbana area. I believe that my experience in
Single- ⟶ taxation as well as my familiarity with the local business
space   community would enable me to contribute to your firm.

I have enclosed a résumé for your examination. I will be
available for an interview any time after midterm examinations,
which end October 25. I look forward to hearing from you.

Compli-   Sincerely yours,
mentary
close   *Sandra Kraft*

Typed   Sandra Kraft
signature   Enc.: Résumé

Additional
data

SAMPLE RÉSUMÉ

KAREN L. OLSON

CURRENT: 3312 Hamilton St. Apt. 18   HOME: 110 Ascot Ct.
          Philadelphia, PA 19104   Harmony, PA 16037
          215-382-0831   412-452-2944
          e-mail kols578@aol.com

EDUCATION

DREXEL UNIVERSITY, Philadelphia, PA 19104
Bachelor of Science in Graphic Design
Anticipated Graduation: June 2000
Cumulative Grade Point Average: 3.2 on a 4.0 scale

COURSE WORK

Corporate Identity, Environmental Graphics, Typography, Photography,
Painting & Printmaking, Sculpture, Computer Imaging, and Art History

EMPLOYMENT EXPERIENCE

UNISYS CORPORATION, Blue Bell, PA 19124
June–September 1999, Cooperative Education
Graphic Designer. Designed interior pages as well as covers for target
marketing brochures. Created various logos and spot art designed for use
on interoffice memos and departmental publications.

CHARMING SHOPPES, INC., Bensalem, PA 19020
June–December 1998, Cooperative Education
Graphic Designer/Fashion Illustrator. Created graphics for future
placement on garments. Did some textile designing. Drew flat
illustrations of garments to scale in computer. Prepared presentation
boards.

THE TRIANGLE. Drexel University, Philadelphia, PA 19104
January 1999–present
Graphics Editor. Design all display advertisements submitted to Drexel's
student-run newspaper.

ACTIVITIES AND AWARDS

Women's Varsity Crew: 1996–present
Kappa Omicron Nu Honor Society, Vice-President: 1999–present
Dean's List: Spring 1999
Graphics Group, Vice-President: 1999–present
Concert and Pep Bands: 1996-1997
Freelance work in corporate art

REFERENCES AND PORTFOLIO

Available upon request.

APPENDIX B

GRAMMAR REVIEW

B1 Parts of Speech

The **part of speech** to which a word belongs depends on its function in a sentence.

(1) Nouns

Nouns name people, places, things, ideas, actions, or qualities.

A **common noun** names any of a class of people, places, or things: *artist, judge, building, event, city.*

A **proper noun,** always capitalized, refers to a particular person, place, or thing: *Mary Cassatt, World Trade Center, Crimean War.*

A **collective noun** designates a group thought of as a unit: *committee, class, family.*

An **abstract noun** refers to an intangible idea or quality: *love, hate, justice, anger, fear, prejudice.*

(2) Pronouns

Pronouns are words used in place of nouns. The noun for which a pronoun stands is called its **antecedent.**

There are eight types of pronouns. Although some of these may have the same form, they are distinguished by their functions.

A **personal pronoun** stands for a person or thing: *I, me, we, us, my, mine, our, ours, you, your, yours, he, she, it, its, him, his, her, hers, they, them, their, theirs.*

They made her an offer she couldn't refuse.

An **indefinite pronoun** does not refer to any particular person or thing, and so it does not require an antecedent. Indefinite pronouns include *another, any, each, few, many, some, nothing, one, anyone, everyone, everybody, everything, someone, something, either,* and *neither.*

Many are called, but few are chosen.

A **reflexive pronoun** ends with -*self* and refers to a recipient of the action that is the same as the actor: *myself, yourself, himself, herself, itself, oneself, themselves, ourselves, yourselves.*

They found themselves in downtown Pittsburgh.

Intensive pronouns have the same form as reflexive pronouns; an intensive pronoun emphasizes a preceding noun or pronoun.

Darrow <u>himself</u> was sure his client was innocent.

A **relative pronoun** introduces an adjective or noun clause in a sentence: *which, who, whom, that, what, whose, whatever, whoever, whomever, whichever.*

People <u>who</u> drink should not drive. (introduces adjective clause)

<u>Whatever</u> happens will be a surprise. (introduces noun clause)

An **interrogative pronoun** introduces a question: *who, which, what, whom, whose, whoever, whatever, whichever.*

<u>Who</u> was that masked man?

A **demonstrative pronoun** points to a particular thing or group of things: *this, that, these, those.*

<u>This</u> is one of Shakespeare's early plays.

A **reciprocal pronoun** denotes a mutual relationship: *each other, one another. Each other* indicates a relationship between two individuals; *one another* denotes a relationship among more than two.

Cathy and I respect <u>each other</u> for our differences.

(3) Verbs

Verbs can be classified into two groups: *main verbs* and *auxiliary verbs.*

Main Verbs **Main verbs** carry most of the meaning in a sentence or clause. Some main verbs are action verbs.

He <u>ran</u> for the train. (action)

Other main verbs function as linking verbs. A **linking verb** links the subject to a **subject complement,** a word or phrase that renames or describes the subject. Linking verbs include *be, become,* and *seem* and verbs that describe sensations—*look, appear, feel, taste, smell,* and so on.

Carbon disulfide <u>smells</u> bad.

Auxiliary Verbs **Auxiliary verbs,** such as *be* and *have,* combine with main verbs to form **verb phrases.** The auxiliary verbs, also known as *helping verbs,* indicate tense, voice, or mood.

[auxiliary]   [main verb]   [auxiliary]   [main verb]

The train <u>has started</u>. We <u>are leaving</u> soon.

[verb phrase]   [verb phrase]

Certain auxiliary verbs, known as **modal auxiliaries,** indicate necessity, possibility, willingness, obligation, or ability. These include *must, shall, might, will, should, can, would, may,* and *could.*

Verbals   **Verbals,** such as *known* or *running* or *to go,* are verb forms that act as adjectives, adverbs, or nouns. A verbal cannot serve as a sentence's main verb unless it is used with one or more auxiliary verbs (*<u>is</u> going*). Verbals include *participles, infinitives,* and *gerunds.*

^{See 6a} *Participles*   Virtually every verb has a **present participle**, which ends in -*ing* (*loving, learning*) and a **past participle**, which ends in -*d* or -*ed* (*agreed, learned*) or is formed irregularly (*gone, begun, written*). Participles may function in a sentence as adjectives or as nouns.

> Twenty brands of <u>running</u> shoes were on display. (participle serves as adjective)

> The <u>wounded</u> were given emergency first aid. (participle serves as noun)

Infinitives   An **infinitive**—the base form of the verb preceded by *to*—may serve as an adjective, an adverb, or a noun.

> Ann Arbor was clearly the place <u>to be</u>. (infinitive serves as adjective)

> Carla went outside <u>to think</u>. (infinitive serves as adverb)

> <u>To win</u> was everything. (infinitive serves as subject)

Gerunds   **Gerunds,** which like present participles end in -*ing,* are always used as nouns.

> <u>Seeing</u> is <u>believing</u>.

> Andrew loves <u>skiing</u>.

(4) Adjectives

Adjectives describe, limit, qualify, or in some other way modify nouns or pronouns.

Descriptive adjectives name a quality of the noun or pronoun they modify.

> After the game, they were <u>exhausted</u>.

> They ordered a <u>chocolate</u> soda and a <u>butterscotch</u> sundae.

When articles, pronouns, numbers, and the like function as adjectives, limiting or qualifying nouns or pronouns, they are referred to as <u>**determiners**</u>.

See
D1.3

(5) Adverbs

Adverbs describe the action of verbs or modify adjectives; other adverbs; or complete phrases, clauses, or sentences. They answer the questions "How?" "Why?" "When?" "Under what conditions?" and "To what extent?"

He walked <u>rather hesitantly</u> toward the front of the room.

Let's meet <u>tomorrow</u> for coffee.

Adverbs that modify other adverbs or adjectives limit or qualify the words they modify.

He pitched an <u>almost perfect</u> game yesterday.

Interrogative Adverbs The **interrogative adverbs** (*how, when, why,* and *where*) introduce questions.

Conjunctive Adverbs **Conjunctive adverbs** act as <u>**transitional words**</u>, joining and relating independent clauses.

See
2b

FREQUENTLY USED CONJUNCTIVE ADVERBS

accordingly	furthermore	meanwhile	similarly
also	hence	moreover	still
anyway	however	nevertheless	then
besides	incidentally	next	thereafter
certainly	indeed	nonetheless	therefore
consequently	instead	now	thus
finally	likewise	otherwise	undoubtedly

---

(6) Prepositions

A **preposition** introduces a noun or pronoun or a phrase or clause functioning in the sentence as a noun. The word or word group that the preposition introduces is its **object.**

$$\text{prep} \quad \text{obj} \qquad \text{prep} \quad \text{obj}$$

They received a postcard <u>from</u> Bobby telling <u>about</u> his trip.

FREQUENTLY USED PREPOSITIONS

about	across	against	among
above	after	along	around

continued on the following page

---

continued from the previous page

as	despite	of	throughout
at	down	off	to
before	during	on	toward
behind	except	onto	under
below	for	out	underneath
beneath	from	outside	until
beside	in	over	up
between	inside	past	upon
beyond	into	regarding	with
by	like	since	within
concerning	near	through	without

(7) Conjunctions

Conjunctions connect words, phrases, clauses, or sentences.

Coordinating Conjunctions **Coordinating conjunctions** (*and, or, but, nor, for, so, yet*) connect words, phrases, or clauses of equal weight.

He had to choose pheasant <u>or</u> venison.

Thoreau wrote *Walden* in 1854, <u>and</u> he died in 1862.

Correlative Conjunctions Always used in pairs, **correlative conjunctions** also link items of equal weight.

<u>Both</u> Hancock <u>and</u> Jefferson signed the Declaration of Independence.

<u>Either</u> I will renew my lease, <u>or</u> I will move.

FREQUENTLY USED CORRELATIVE CONJUNCTIONS

both . . . and	neither . . . nor
either . . . or	not only . . . but also
just as . . . so	whether . . . or

Subordinating Conjunctions Words such as *since, because,* and *although* are **subordinating conjunctions.** They introduce adverb clauses and thus connect the sentence's independent (main) clause to a dependent (subordinate) clause to form a <u>complex sentence</u>.

See
9a2

<u>Although</u> people may feel healthy, they can still have medical problems.

It is best to diagram your garden <u>before</u> you start to plant.

(8) Interjections

Interjections **Interjections** are words used as exclamations to express emotion: *Oh! Ouch! Wow! Alas! Hey!* They may be set off by commas or, for greater emphasis, by an exclamation point.

B2 Sentences

(1) Basic Sentence Elements

A **sentence** is an independent grammatical unit that contains a <u>subject</u> and a <u>predicate</u> and expresses a complete thought.

<u>The quick brown fox</u> <u>jumped over the lazy dog</u>.

<u>It</u> <u>came from outer space</u>.

(2) Basic Sentence Patterns

A **simple sentence** consists of at least one subject and one predicate. Simple sentences conform to one of five patterns.

Subject + Intransitive verb (s + v)

   s   v
<u>Stock prices</u> <u>may fall</u>.

Subject + Transitive Verb + Direct Object (s + v + do)

   s   v   do
<u>Van Gogh</u> <u>created</u> *The Starry Night*.

   s   v   do
<u>Caroline</u> <u>saved</u> Jake.

Subject + Transitive Verb + Direct Object + Object Complement (s + v + do + oc)

s v   do   oc
<u>I</u> <u>found</u> the exam easy.

   s   v   do   oc
<u>The class</u> <u>elected</u> Bridget treasurer.

Subject + Linking Verb + Subject Complement (s + v + sc)

    s   v   sc
<u>The injection</u> <u>was</u> painless.

   s   v   sc
<u>Tony Blair</u> <u>became</u> prime minister.

Subject + Transitive Verb + Indirect Object + Direct Object (s + v + io + do)

   s   v   io   do
<u>Cyrano</u> <u>wrote</u> Roxanne a poem. (Cyrano wrote a poem for Roxanne.)

   s   v   io   do
<u>Hester</u> <u>gave</u> Pearl a kiss. (Hester gave a kiss to Pearl.)

(3) Phrases and Clauses

A **phrase** is a group of related words that lacks a subject or predicate or both and functions as a single part of speech. It cannot stand alone as a sentence.

A **verb phrase** consists of a **main verb** and all its auxiliary verbs. (Time *is flying.*) A **noun phrase** includes a noun or pronoun plus all related modifiers. (I'll climb *the highest mountain.*)

See
B1.6

A **prepositional phrase** consists of a <u>**preposition**</u>, its object, and any modifiers of that object (the ethical implications *of the animal studies*).

See
B1.3

A **verbal phrase** consists of a <u>**verbal**</u> and its related objects, modifiers, or complements. A verbal phrase may be a **participial phrase** (*encouraged by the voter turnout*), a **gerund phrase** (*taking it easy*), or an **infinitive phrase** (*to evaluate the evidence*).

An **absolute phrase** usually consists of a noun and a participle, accompanied by modifiers. It modifies an entire independent clause.

> <u>Their toes tapping</u>, they watched the auditions.

A **clause** is a group of related words that includes a subject and a predicate. An **independent** (main) **clause** may stand alone as a sentence, but a **dependent** (subordinate) **clause** cannot. It must always be combined with an independent clause to form a <u>**complex sentence**</u>.

See
9a2

> [Lucretia Mott was an abolitionist.] [She was also a pioneer for women's rights.] (two independent clauses)

> [Lucretia Mott was an abolitionist] [who was also a pioneer for women's rights.] (independent clause, dependent clause)

Dependent clauses may be adjective, adverb, or noun clauses.

Adjective clauses, sometimes called **relative clauses,** modify nouns or pronouns and always follow the nouns or pronouns they modify. They are introduced by relative pronouns—*that, what, which, who,* and so forth—or by the adverbs *where* and *when.*

> Celeste's grandparents, <u>who were born in Romania</u>, speak little English.

Adverb clauses modify verbs, adjectives, adverbs, entire phrases, or independent clauses. They are always introduced by subordinating conjunctions.

> Mark will go <u>wherever there's a party.</u>

Noun clauses function as subjects, objects, or complements. A noun clause may be introduced by a relative pronoun or by *whether, when, where, why,* or *how.*

<u>What you see</u> is <u>what you get</u>.

(4) Types of Sentences

A **simple sentence** is a single independent clause. A simple sentence can consist of just a subject and a predicate.

<u>Jessica</u> <u>fell</u>.

Or, a simple sentence can be expanded.

Jessica fell in love with Henry Goodyear.

A <u>**compound sentence**</u> consists of two or more simple sentences linked by a comma and a coordinating conjunction, by a semicolon (alone or with a transitional word or phrase), or by a colon. See 9a1

[The moon rose in the sky], <u>and</u> [the stars shone brightly].

[José wanted to spend a quiet afternoon]; <u>however</u>, [his aunt surprised him with a new set of plans.]

A <u>**complex sentence**</u> consists of an independent clause along with one or more dependent clauses. See 9a2

  Independent clause   Dependent clause
[It was hard for us to believe] [that anyone could be so cruel].

A **compound-complex sentence** is a compound sentence—made up of at least two independent clauses—that also includes at least one dependent clause.

[My mother always worried] [when my father had to work late], and [she could rarely sleep more than a few minutes at a time].

Sentences can also be classified according to their function. **Declarative sentences** make statements; they are the most common. **Interrogative sentences** pose questions, usually by inverting standard subject-verb order (often with an interrogative word) or adding a form of *do* (*Is Maggie at home? Where is Maggie? Does Maggie live here?*). **Imperative sentences** express commands or requests, using the second-person singular of the verb and generally omitting the pronoun subject *you* (*Go to your room. Please believe me.*). **Exclamatory sentences** express strong emotion and end with an exclamation point (*The killing must stop now!*).

A GLOSSARY OF USAGE

This glossary of usage lists words and phrases that are often troublesome for writers.

a, an   Use *a* before words that begin with consonants and words that have initial vowels that sound like consonants: *a* person, *a* one-horse carriage, *a* uniform. Use *an* before words that begin with vowels and words that begin with a silent *h: an* artist, *an* honest person.

accept, except   *Accept* is a verb that means "to receive"; *except* as a preposition or conjunction means "other than" and as a verb means "to leave out": The auditors will *accept* all your claims *except* the last two. Some businesses are *excepted* from the regulation.

advice, advise   *Advice* is a noun meaning "opinion or information offered"; *advise* is a verb that means "to offer advice to": The broker *advised* her client to take his attorney's *advice.*

affect, effect   *Affect* is a verb meaning "to influence"; *effect* can be a verb or a noun—as a verb it means "to bring about," and as a noun it means "result": We know how the drug *affects* patients immediately, but little is known of its long-term *effects.* The arbitrator tried to *effect* a settlement between the parties.

all ready, already   *All ready* means "completely prepared"; *Already* means "by or before this or that time": I was *all ready* to help, but it was *already* too late.

all right, alright   Although the use of *alright* is increasing, current usage calls for *all right.*

allusion, illusion   An *allusion* is a reference or hint; an *illusion* is something that is not what it seems: The poem makes an *allusion* to the Pandora myth. The shadows created an optical *illusion.*

a lot   *A lot* is always two words.

among, between   *Among* refers to groups of more than two things; *between* refers to just two things: The three parties agreed *among* themselves to settle the case. There will be a brief intermission *between* the two acts.

amount, number   *Amount* refers to a quantity that cannot be counted; *number* refers to things that can be counted: Even a small *amount* of caffeine can be harmful. Seeing their commander fall, a large *number* of troops ran to his aid.

an, a   See **a, an.**

and/or In business or technical writing, use *and/or* when either or both of the items it connects can apply. In college writing, however, the use of *and/or* should generally be avoided.

as . . . as . . . In such constructions, *as* signals a comparison; therefore, you must always use the second *as: East of Eden* is *as* long *as* if not longer than *The Grapes of Wrath.*

as, like *As* can be used as a conjunction (to introduce a complete clause) or as a preposition; *like* should be used as a preposition only: In *The Scarlet Letter* Hawthorne uses imagery *as* (not *like*) he does in his other works. After classes he works *as* a manager of a fast-food restaurant. Writers *like* Carl Sandburg appear once in a generation.

at, to Many people use the prepositions *at* and *to* after *where* in conversation: *Where* are you working *at? Where* are you going *to?* This usage is redundant and should not be used in college writing.

awhile, a while *Awhile* is an adverb; *a while,* which consists of an article and a noun, is used as the object of a preposition: Before we continue we will rest *awhile.* (modifies the verb *rest*); Before we continue we will rest for *a while.* (object of the preposition *for*)

bad, badly *Bad* is an adjective, and *badly* is an adverb: The school board decided that *Huckleberry Finn* was a *bad* book. American automobile makers did not do *badly* this year. After verbs that refer to any of the senses or after any other linking verb, use the adjective form: He looked *bad.* He felt *bad.* It seemed *bad.*

being as, being that These awkward phrases add unnecessary words and weaken your writing. Use *because* instead.

beside, besides *Beside* is a preposition meaning "next to"; *besides* can be either a preposition meaning "except" or "other than," or an adverb meaning "as well": *Beside* the tower was a wall that ran the length of the city. *Besides* its industrial uses, laser technology has many other applications. Edison invented not only the lightbulb but the phonograph *besides.*

between, among See **among, between.**

bring, take *Bring* means to transport from a farther place to a nearer place; *take* means to carry or convey from a nearer place to a farther one: *Bring* me a souvenir from your trip. *Take* this message to the general and wait for a reply.

can, may *Can* denotes ability, and *may* indicates permission: If you *can* play, you *may* use my piano.

capital, capitol *Capital* refers to a city that is an official seat of government; *capitol* refers to a building in which a legislature meets: Washington, DC, is the *capital* of the United States. When we were there, we visited the *Capitol* building.

center around This imprecise phrase is acceptable in speech and informal writing but not in college writing. Use *center on* instead.

cite, site   *Cite* is a verb meaning "to quote as an authority or example"; *site* is a noun meaning "a place or setting": Jeff *cited* five sources in his research paper. The builder cleared the *site* for the new bank.

climactic, climatic   *Climactic* means "of or related to a climax"; *climatic* means "of or related to climate": The *climactic* moment of the movie occurs unexpectedly. If scientists are correct, the *climatic* conditions of Earth are changing.

coarse, course   *Coarse* is an adjective meaning "inferior" or "having a rough, uneven texture"; *course* is a noun meaning "a route or path," "an area on which a sport is played," or "a unit of study": *Coarse* sandpaper is used to smooth the surface. The *course* of true love never runs smoothly. Last semester I had to drop a *course*.

compare to, compare with   *Compare to* means "to liken" or "to represent as similar"; *compare with* means "to examine in order to find ways in which two things are similar or different": Shall I *compare* you *to* a summer's day? Jane *compared* the paintings of Cézanne *with* those of Magritte.

complement, compliment   *Complement* means "to complete or add to"; *compliment* means "to give praise": A double-blind study would *complement* their preliminary research. My instructor *complimented* me on my improvement.

conscious, conscience   *Conscious* is an adjective meaning "having one's mental faculties awake"; *conscience* is a noun that means the moral sense of right and wrong: The patient will remain *conscious* during the procedure. His *conscience* wouldn't allow him to lie.

continual, continuous   *Continual* means "recurring at intervals"; *continuous* refers to an action that occurs without interruption: A pulsar is a star that emits a *continual* stream of electromagnetic radiation. (It emits radiation at regular intervals.) A small battery allows the watch to run *continuously* for five years. (It runs without stopping.)

could of, should of, would of   The contractions *could've*, *should've*, and *would've* are often misspelled as the nonstandard constructions *could of, should of,* and *would of.* Use *could have, should have,* and *would have* in college writing.

council, counsel   A *council* is "a body of people who serve in a legislative or advisory capacity"; *counsel* means "to offer advice or guidance": The city *council* argued about the proposed ban on smoking. The judge *counseled* the couple to settle their differences.

couple of   *Couple* means "a pair," but *couple of* is used colloquially to mean "several" or "a few." In your college writing, specify "four points" or "two examples" rather than using "a couple of."

criterion, criteria   *Criteria,* from the Greek, is the plural of *criterion,* meaning "standard for judgment": Of all the *criteria* for hiring graduating seniors, class rank is the most important *criterion.*

data   *Data* is the plural of the Latin *datum,* meaning "fact." In everyday speech and writing *data* is used for both singular and plural. In college writing, you should use *data* only for the plural: The *data* discussed in this section *are* summarized in Appendix A.

different from, different than   *Different than* is widely used in American speech. In college writing, use *different from.*

discreet, discrete   *Discreet* means "careful or prudent"; *discrete* means "separate or individually distinct": Because Madame Bovary was not *discreet,* her reputation suffered. Atoms can be broken into hundreds of *discrete* particles.

disinterested, uninterested   *Disinterested* means "objective" or "capable of making an impartial judgment"; *uninterested* means "indifferent or unconcerned": The American judicial system depends on *disinterested* jurors. Finding no treasure, Hernando de Soto was *uninterested* in going farther.

don't, doesn't   *Don't* is the contraction of *do not; doesn't* is the contraction of *does not.* Do not confuse the two: My dog *doesn't* (not *don't*) like to walk in the rain.

effect, affect   See **affect, effect.**

e.g.   *E.g.* is an abbreviation for the Latin *exempli gratia,* meaning "for example" or "for instance." In college writing, do not use *e.g.* Instead, use its English equivalent.

emigrate from, immigrate to   To *emigrate* is "to leave one's country and settle in another"; to *immigrate* is "to come to another country and reside there." The noun forms of these words are *emigrant* and *immigrant*: My great-grandfather *emigrated from* Warsaw along with many other *emigrants* from Poland. Many people *immigrate* to the United States for economic reasons, but such *immigrants* still face great challenges.

eminent, imminent   *Eminent* is an adjective meaning "standing above others" or "prominent"; *imminent* means "about to occur": Oliver Wendell Holmes, Jr., was an *eminent* jurist. In ancient times, a comet signaled *imminent* disaster.

enthused   *Enthused,* a colloquial form of *enthusiastic,* should not be used in college writing.

etc.   *Etc.,* the abbreviation of *et cetera,* means "and the rest." Do not use it in your college writing. Instead, say "and so on" or, better, specify exactly what *etc.* stands for.

everyday, every day   *Everyday* is an adjective that means "ordinary" or "commonplace"; *every day* means "occurring daily": In the Gettysburg Address, Lincoln used *everyday* language. She exercises almost *every day.*

everyone, every one   *Everyone* is an indefinite pronoun meaning "every person"; *every one* means "every individual or thing in a particular group": *Everyone* seems happier in the spring. *Every one* of the packages had been opened.

except, accept   See **accept, except.**

explicit, implicit   *Explicit* means "expressed or stated directly"; *implicit* means "implied" or "expressed or stated indirectly": The director *explicitly* warned the actors to be on time for rehearsals. Her *implicit* message was that lateness would not be tolerated.

farther, further   *Farther* designates distance; *further* designates degree: I have traveled *farther* from home than any of my relatives. Critics charge that welfare subsidies encourage *further* dependence.

fewer, less   Use *fewer* with nouns that can be counted: *fewer* books, *fewer* people, *fewer* dollars. Use *less* with quantities that cannot be counted: *less* pain, *less* power, *less* enthusiasm.

firstly (secondly, thirdly, . . .)   Archaic forms meaning "in the first . . . second . . . third place." Use *first, second, third.*

further, farther   See **farther, further.**

good, well   *Good* is an adjective, never an adverb: She is a *good* swimmer. *Well* can function as an adverb or as an adjective. As an adverb it means "in a good manner": She swam *well* (not *good*) in the meet. *Well* is used as an adjective with verbs that denote a state of being or feeling. Here *well* can mean "in good health": I feel *well.*

got to   *Got to* is not acceptable in college writing. To indicate obligation, use *have to, has to,* or *must.*

hanged, hung   Both *hanged* and *hung* are past participles of *hang. Hanged* is used to refer to executions; *hung* is used to mean "suspended": Billy Budd was *hanged* for killing the master-at-arms. The stockings were *hung* by the chimney with care.

he, she   Traditionally *he* has been used in the generic sense to refer to both males and females. To acknowledge the equality of the sexes, however, avoid the generic *he.* Use plural pronouns whenever possible. See **14d.2.**

hopefully   The adverb *hopefully,* meaning "in a hopeful manner," should modify a verb, an adjective, or another adverb. Do not use *hopefully* as a sentence modifier meaning "it is hoped." Rather than "*Hopefully,* scientists will soon discover a cure for AIDS," write "Scientists *hope* they will soon discover a cure for AIDS."

i.e.   *I.e.* is an abbreviation for the Latin *id est,* meaning "that is." In college writing, do not use *i.e.* Instead, use its English equivalent.

if, whether   When asking indirect questions or expressing doubt, use *whether:* He asked *whether* (not *if*) the flight would be delayed. The flight attendant was not sure *whether* (not *if*) it would be delayed.

illusion, allusion   See **allusion, illusion.**

immigrate to, emigrate from   See **emigrate from, immigrate to.**

implicit, explicit   See **explicit, implicit.**

imply, infer   *Imply* means "to hint" or "to suggest"; *infer* means "to conclude from": Mark Antony *implied* that the conspirators had murdered Caesar. The crowd *inferred* his meaning and called for justice.

infer, imply   See **imply, infer.**

inside of, outside of   *Of* is unnecessary when *inside* and *outside* are used as prepositions. *Inside of* is colloquial in references to time: He waited *inside* (not *inside of*) the coffee shop. He could run a mile in *under* (not *inside of*) eight minutes.

irregardless, regardless   *Irregardless* is a nonstandard version of *regardless*. Use *regardless* instead.

is when, is where   These constructions are faulty when they appear in definitions: A playoff *is* an additional game played to establish the winner of a tie. (not "A playoff *is when* an additional game is played. . . .")

its, it's   *Its* is a possessive pronoun; *it's* is a contraction of *it is*: *It's* no secret that the bank is out to protect *its* assets.

kind of, sort of   *Kind of* and *sort of* to mean "rather" or "somewhat" are colloquial and should not appear in college writing: It is well known that Napoleon was *rather* (not *kind of*) short.

lay, lie   See **lie, lay.**

leave, let   *Leave* means "to go away from" or "to let remain"; *let* means "to allow" or "to permit": *Let* (not *leave*) me give you a hand.

less, fewer   See **fewer, less.**

let, leave   See **leave, let.**

lie, lay   *Lie* is an intransitive verb (one that does not take an object) that means "to recline." Its principal forms are *lie, lay, lain, lying*: Each afternoon she would *lie* in the sun and listen to the surf. *As I Lay Dying* is a novel by William Faulkner. By 1871 Troy had *lain* undisturbed for two thousand years. The painting shows a nude *lying* on a couch. *Lay* is a transitive verb (one that takes an object) meaning "to put" or "to place." Its principal forms are *lay, laid, laid, laying*: The Federalist Papers *lay* the foundation for American conservatism. In October of 1781 the British *laid* down their arms and surrendered. He had *laid* his money on the counter before leaving. We watched the stonemasons *laying* a wall.

like, as   See **as, like.**

loose, lose   *Loose* is an adjective meaning "not rigidly fastened or securely attached"; *lose* is a verb meaning "to misplace": The marble facing of the building became *loose* and fell to the sidewalk. After only two drinks, most people *lose* their ability to judge distance.

lots, lots of, a lot of   These words are colloquial substitutes for *many, much,* or *a great deal of.* Avoid their use in college writing: The students had *many* (not *lots of* or *a lot of*) options for essay topics.

man   Like the generic pronoun *he, man* has been used in English to denote members of both sexes. This usage is being replaced by *human beings, people,* or similar terms that do not specify gender. See **14d.2.**

may, can   See **can, may.**

may be, maybe   *May be* is a verb phrase; *maybe* is an adverb meaning "perhaps": She *may be* the smartest student in the class. *Maybe* her experience has given her an advantage.

media, medium   *Medium,* meaning a "means of conveying or broadcasting something," is singular; *media* is the plural form and requires a plural verb: The *media* have distorted the issue.

might have, might of   *Might of* is a nonstandard spelling of the contraction of *might have* (*might've*).

number, amount   See **amount, number.**

OK, O.K., okay   All three spellings are acceptable, but this term should be avoided in college writing. Replace it with a more specific word or words: The instructor's lecture was *adequate* (not *okay*), if uninspiring.

outside of, inside of   See **inside of, outside of.**

passed, past   *Passed* is the past tense of the verb *pass; past* means "belonging to a former time" or "no longer current": The car must have been going eighty miles per hour when it *passed* us. In the envelope was a bill marked *past* due.

percent, percentage   *Percent* indicates a part of a hundred when a specific number is referred to: "*10 percent* of his salary." *Percentage* is used when no specific number is referred to: "a *percentage* of next year's receipts." In technical and business writing it is permissible to use the % sign after percentages you are comparing. Write out *percent* in college writing.

phenomenon, phenomena   A *phenomenon* is a single observable fact or event. It can also refer to a rare or significant occurrence. *Phenomena* is the plural form and requires a plural verb: Many supposedly paranormal *phenomena* are easily explained.

plus   As a preposition, *plus* means "in addition to." Avoid using *plus* as a substitute for *and:* Include the principal, *plus* the interest, in your calculations. Your quote was too high; moreover (not *plus*), it was inaccurate.

precede, proceed   *Precede* means "to go or come before"; *proceed* means "to go forward in an orderly way": Robert Frost's *North of Boston* was *preceded* by an earlier volume. In 1532 Francisco Pizarro landed at Tumbes and *proceeded* south.

principal, principle   As a noun, *principal* means "a sum of money (minus interest) invested or lent" or "a person in the leading position"; as an adjective it means "most important." A *principle* is a rule of conduct or a basic truth: He wanted to reduce the *principal* of the loan. The *principal* of the high school is a talented administrator. Women are the *principal* wage earners in many American households. The Constitution embodies certain fundamental *principles.*

quote, quotation   *Quote* is a verb. *Quotation* is a noun. In formal writing situations, do not use *quote* as a shortened form of *quotation:* He included several *quotations* (not *quotes*) from experts.

raise, rise   *Raise* is a transitive verb, and *rise* is an intransitive verb—that is, *raise* takes an object, and *rise* does not: My grandparents *raised* a large family. The sun will *rise* at 6:12 this morning.

real, really   *Real* means "genuine" or "authentic"; *really* means "actually." In your college writing, do not use *real* as an adjective meaning "very."

reason is that, reason is because   *Reason* should be used with *that* and not with *because,* which is redundant: The *reason* he left *is that* (not *is because*) you insulted him.

regardless, irregardless   See **irregardless, regardless.**

respectably, respectfully, respectively   *Respectably* means "worthy of respect"; *respectfully* means "giving honor or deference"; *respectively* means "in the order given": He skated quite *respectably* at his first Olympics. The seminar taught us to treat others *respectfully.* The first- and second-place winners were Tai and Kim, *respectively.*

rise, raise   See **raise, rise.**

set, sit   *Set* means "to put down" or "to lay." Its principal forms are *set* and *setting:* After rocking the baby to sleep, he *set* her down carefully in her crib. *Sit* means "to assume a sitting position." Its principal forms are *sit, sat, sat,* and *sitting:* Many children *sit* in front of the television five to six hours a day.

shall, will   *Will* has all but replaced *shall* to express all future action.

should of   See **could of, should of, would of.**

since   Do not use *since* for *because* if there is any chance of confusion. In the sentence "*Since* President Nixon traveled to China, trade between China and the United States has increased," *since* could mean either "from the time that" or "because."

sit, set   See **set, sit.**

so   Avoid using *so* alone as a vague intensifier meaning "very" or "extremely." Follow *so* with *that* and a clause that describes the result: She was *so* pleased with their work *that* she took them out to lunch.

sometime, sometimes, some time   *Sometime* means "at some time in the future"; *sometimes* means "now and then"; *some time* means "a period of time": The president will address Congress *sometime* next week. All automobiles, no matter how reliable, *sometimes* need repairs. It has been *some time* since I read that book.

sort of, kind of   See **kind of, sort of.**

stationary, stationery   *Stationary* means "staying in one place"; *stationery* means "materials for writing" or "letter paper": The communications satellite appears to be *stationary* in the sky. The secretaries supply departmental offices with *stationery*.

supposed to, used to   *Supposed to* and *used to* are often misspelled. Both verbs require the final *d* to indicate past tense.

take, bring   See **bring, take.**

than, then   *Than* is a conjunction used to indicate a comparison; *then* is an adverb indicating time: The new shopping center is bigger *than* the old one. He did his research; *then* he wrote a report.

that, which, who   Use *that* or *which* when referring to a thing; use *who* when referring to a person: It was a speech *that* inspired many. The movie, *which* was a huge success, failed to impress her. Anyone *who* (not *that*) takes the course will benefit.

their, there, they're   *Their* is a possessive pronoun; *there* indicates place and is also used in the expressions *there is* and *there are*; *they're* is a contraction of *they are*: Watson and Crick did *their* DNA work at Cambridge University. I love New York, but I wouldn't want to live *there*. *There* is nothing we can do to resurrect an extinct species. When *they're* well treated, ferrets make excellent pets.

themselves; theirselves, theirself   *Theirselves* and *theirself* are nonstandard variants of *themselves*.

then, than   See **than, then.**

till, until, 'til   *Till* and *until* have the same meaning, and both are acceptable. *Until* is preferred in college writing. *'Til*, a contraction of *until*, should be avoided.

to, at   See **at, to.**

to, too, two   *To* is a preposition that indicates direction; *too* is an adverb that means "also" or "more than is needed"; *two* expresses the number 2: Last year we flew from New York *to* California. "Tippecanoe and Tyler, *too*" was Harrison's campaign slogan. The plot was *too* complicated for the average reader. Just north of *Two* Rivers, Wisconsin, is a petrified forest.

try to, try and   *Try and* is the colloquial equivalent of the more formal *try to*: He decided to *try to* (not *try and*) do better.

-type   Deleting this empty suffix eliminates clutter and clarifies meaning: Found in the wreckage was an *incendiary* (not *incendiary-type*) device.

uninterested, disinterested   See **disinterested, uninterested.**

unique   Because *unique* means "the only one," not "remarkable" or "unusual," you should never use constructions like "the most unique" or "very unique."

until   See **till, until, 'til.**

used to   See **supposed to, used to.**

utilize   In most cases, it is best to replace *utilize* with *use* (*utilize* often sounds pretentious).

wait for, wait on   To *wait for* means "to defer action until something occurs." To *wait on* means "to act as a waiter": I am *waiting for* (not *on*) dinner.

weather, whether   *Weather* is a noun meaning "the state of the atmosphere"; *whether* is a conjunction used to introduce an alternative: The *weather* outside is frightful, but the fire inside is delightful. It is doubtful *whether* we will be able to ski tomorrow.

well, good   See **good, well.**

were, we're   *Were* is a verb; *we're* is the contraction of *we are:* The Trojans *were* asleep when the Greeks attacked. We must act now if *we're* going to succeed.

whether, if   See **if, whether.**

which, who, that   See **that, which, who.**

who, whom   When a pronoun serves as the subject of its clause, use *who* or *whoever;* when it functions in a clause as an object, use *whom* or *whomever:* Sarah, *who* is studying ancient civilizations, would like to visit Greece. Sarah, *whom* I met in France, wants me to travel to Greece with her. To determine which to use at the beginning of a question, use a personal pronoun to answer the question: *Who* tried to call me? *He* called. (subject); *Whom* do you want for the job? I want *her.* (object)

who's, whose   *Who's* means "who is"; *whose* indicates possession: *Who's* going to take calculus? The writer *whose* book was in the window was autographing copies.

will, shall   See **shall, will.**

would of   See **could of, should of, would of.**

your, you're   *Your* indicates possession, and *you're* is the contraction of *you are:* You can improve *your* stamina by jogging two miles a day. *You're* certain to be the winner.

APPENDIX D

ENGLISH FOR SPEAKERS OF OTHER LANGUAGES

✔ CHECKLIST: ENGLISH LANGUAGE BASICS

✔ **Words in English sentences may change their form according to their function.** For example, verbs change form to communicate whether an action is taking place in the past, present, or future.

✔ **In English, context is extremely important to understanding function.** In the following sentences, for instance, the very same words can perform different functions according to their relationships to other words.

Juan and I are taking a <u>walk</u>. (*Walk* is a noun, a direct object of the verb *taking*, with an article, *a*, attached to it.)

If you <u>walk</u> whenever you can instead of driving, you will help conserve the Earth's resources. (*Walk* is a verb, the predicate of the subject *you*.)

See
Ch. 21

✔ **Spelling in English is not always phonetic and sometimes may seem illogical.** <u>Spelling</u> in English is often a matter of memorization, not sounding out the word phonetically. For example, the "ough" sound in the words *tough, though,* and *thought* is pronounced quite differently in each case. Spelling in English may be related more to the history of the word and its origins in other languages than to the way the word is pronounced.

✔ **Word order is extremely important in English sentences.** In English sentences, word order may indicate which word is the subject of the sentence and which is the object, whether the sentence is a question or a statement, and so on.

D1 Nouns

If a noun names one thing, it is a **singular** noun; if a noun names many things, it is a **plural** noun.

See
21b7

(1) Noncount Nouns

Some English nouns do not have a plural form. These are called **noncount nouns** because what they name cannot be counted.

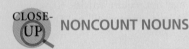

CLOSE-UP NONCOUNT NOUNS

The following commonly used nouns are noncount nouns. These words have no plural forms. Therefore, you should never add -*s* to them.

advice	homework
clothing	information
education	knowledge
equipment	luggage
evidence	merchandise
furniture	revenge

(2) Articles with Nouns

English has two **articles:** *a* and *the*. *A* is called the **indefinite** article; *the* is the **definite article.** *A* is replaced by *an* if the word that follows begins with a *vowel* (*a, e, i, o,* or *u*) or with a vowel *sound: a* book, *an* apple, *an* honor. If the vowel is pronounced like a consonant, use *a: a one-time offer.*

Use an **indefinite article** with a noun when the reader has no reason to be familiar with the noun you are naming—when you are introducing the noun for the first time, for example. To say, "There was a sidewalk in front of *a* building," signals to the audience that you are introducing the idea of the building for the first time. The building is indefinite, or not specific, until it has been identified.

Use the **definite article** when the noun you are naming has already been introduced. To say, "There was a sidewalk in front of *the* building," signals to readers that you are referring to the same building you mentioned earlier.

> ### CLOSE-UP USING ARTICLES WITH NOUNS
>
> There are two main exceptions to the rules governing the use of articles with nouns.
>
> - **Plural nouns** do not require **indefinite articles:** "I love horses," not "I love a horses." (Plural nouns do, however, require definite articles: "I love <u>the</u> horses in the national park near my house.")
> - **Noncount nouns** may not require articles: "Love conquers all," not "<u>A</u> love conquers all" or "<u>The</u> love conquers all."

(3) Using Other Determiners with Nouns

See
D4

Determiners are words that function as <u>adjectives</u> to limit or qualify the meaning of nouns. In addition to articles, **demonstrative pronouns, possessive nouns and pronouns, numbers** (both **cardinal** and **ordinal**), and other words indicating *number* and *order* can function in this way.

1. **Demonstrative pronouns** (*this, that, these, those*) communicate

   - the relative nearness or farness of the noun from the speaker's position (*this* and *these* for things that are *near*, *that* and *those* for things that are *far*): *this* book on my desk, *that* book on your desk; *these* shoes on my feet, *those* shoes in my closet.
   - the *number* of things indicated (*this* and *that* for *singular* nouns, *these* and *those* for *plural* nouns): *this* (or *that*) flower in the vase, *those* flowers in the garden.

2. **Possessive nouns** and **possessive pronouns** (*Ashraf's, his, their*) show who or what the noun belongs to: *Maria's* courage, *everybody's* fears, the *country's* natural resources, *my* personality, *our* groceries.

3. **Cardinal** numbers (*three, fifty, a thousand*) and **ordinal** numbers (*first, tenth, thirtieth*) indicate how many of the noun you mean and in what order the noun appears among other items: *seven* continents, *third* planet.

4. Words other than numbers may indicate **amount** (*many, few*) and **order** (*next, last*) and function in the same ways as cardinal and ordinal numbers: *few* opportunities, *last* chance.

D2 Pronouns

Any English noun may be replaced by a <u>**pronoun**</u>. Pronouns enable you to avoid repeating a noun over and over. For example, *doctor* may be replaced by *he* or *she*, *books* by *them*, and *computer* by *it*.

See
B1.2

D3 Verbs

(1) Person and Number

<u>**Person**</u> refers to *who* or *what* is performing the action of the verb (for example, *myself*, *you*, or someone else), and <u>**number**</u> refers to *how many* people or things are performing the action (one or more than one). Unless you use the correct person and number in the verbs in your sentences, you will confuse your English-speaking audience by communicating meanings you do not intend.

See
11a.4

(2) Tense

<u>**Tense**</u> refers to *when* the action of the verb takes place. For example, adding *-ed* to many English verbs creates a past tense and places the action of the verb in the past. One problem that many nonnative speakers of English have with English verb tenses results from the large number of <u>**irregular verbs**</u> in English. For example, the first-person singular present tense of *to be* is not "I be" but "I am," and the past tense is not "I beed" but "I was."

See
6b

See
6a

(3) Auxiliary Verbs

Meaning is also communicated in English through the use of <u>**auxiliary verbs**</u> (also known as **helping verbs**), such as forms of the verbs *to be* and *to have* ("Julio *is taking* a vacation," "I *have been* tired lately."), and also <u>**modal auxiliaries**</u> such as *would*, *should*, and *can* ("We *should conserve* more of our resources," "You *can succeed* if you try").

See
B1.3

See
B1.3

CLOSE-UP AUXILIARY VERBS

Only auxiliary verbs, not the verbs they "help," change form to indicate person, number, and tense.

We ~~have~~ ^{had} to ~~went~~ ^{go} downtown yesterday. (Only the auxiliary verb *had* should be in the past tense.)

See
6b

(4) Verb Tense

Some nonnative speakers of English use <u>**verb tenses**</u> that are more complicated than they need to be. Such speakers may do this because their native language uses more complicated tenses where English does not or because they are nervous about using simple tenses and "overcorrect" their verbs into complicated tenses.

Specifically, nonnative speakers tend to use **progressive** (present and past) verb forms instead of **simple** (present and past) verb forms, and **perfect** (present and past) verb forms instead of **simple** (present and past) verb forms. To communicate your ideas clearly to an English-speaking audience, choose the simplest possible verb tense.

(5) Double Negatives

The meaning of a verb may be made negative in English in a variety of ways, chiefly by adding the words *not* or *does not* to the verb (is, *is not,* can ski, *can't* ski; drives a car, *does not* drive a car).

CLOSE-UP CORRECTING DOUBLE NEGATIVES

A **double negative** occurs when the meaning of a verb is negated not just once but twice.

Henry doesn't have ~~no~~ friends at all. (*or* Henry ~~doesn't~~ ~~have~~ no friends at all.) [with "any" above "no" and "has" above "have"]

I looked for articles in the library, but there weren't none. (*or* I looked for articles in the library, but there weren't ~~none~~.) [with "any" above "none"]

D4 Adjectives and Adverbs

Adjectives in English usually appear *before* the nouns they describe. A native speaker of English would not say, "*Cars red and black* are involved in more accidents than *cars blue or green*," but would say instead, "*Red and black cars* are involved in more accidents than *blue or green cars.*"

Adverbs may appear *before or after* the verbs they describe, but they should be placed as close to the verb as possible: not "I *told* John that I couldn't meet him for lunch *politely*," but "I *politely told* John that I couldn't meet him for lunch" or "I *told* John *politely* that I couldn't meet him for lunch." When an adverb describes an adjective or another adverb, it usually comes *before* the adjective or the adverb: "The essay has *basically sound* logic."

A single noun may be described by more than one adjective, perhaps even by a whole list of adjectives in a row. Given a list of three or four adjectives, most native speakers would arrange them in a sentence in the same order. If shoes are to be described as *green* and *big*, numbering *two*, and of the type worn for playing *tennis*, a native speaker would say "two big green tennis shoes." Generally, the adjectives that are most important in completing the meaning of the noun are placed closest to the noun.

CLOSE-UP   ORDER OF ADJECTIVES

1. articles (*a, the*), demonstratives (*this, those*), and possessives (*his, our, Maria's, everybody's*)
2. amounts (*one, five, many, few*), order (*first, next, last*)
3. personal opinions (*nice, ugly, crowded, pitiful*)
4. sizes and shapes (*small, tall, straight, crooked*)
5. age (*young, old, modern, ancient*)
6. colors (*black, white, red, blue, dark, light*)
7. nouns functioning as adjectives to form a unit with the noun (*soccer* ball, *cardboard* box, *history* class)

D5 Prepositions

In English, **prepositions** (such as *to, from, at, with, among, between*) give meaning to nouns by linking them with other words and other parts of the sentence. Prepositions convey several different kinds of information.

See
B1.6

- relations to **time** (*at* nine o'clock, *in* five minutes, *for* a month)
- relations of **place** (*in* the classroom, *at* the library, *beside* the chair) and **direction** (*to* the market, *onto* the stage, *toward* the freeway)
- relations of **association** (go *with* someone, the tip *of* the iceberg)
- relations of **purpose** (working *for* money, dieting *to* lose weight)

In some languages, prepositions may be used in quite different ways, may exist in forms quite different from English, or may not exist at all. Speakers of languages with prepositions very similar to those in English—especially Romance languages such as Spanish, French, and Italian—have a different problem.

They may be tempted to translate prepositional phrases directly from their own language into English.

CLOSE-UP: PREPOSITIONS IN IDIOMATIC EXPRESSIONS

Common nonnative speaker usage	Native speaker usage
according *with*	according *to*
apologize *at*	apologize *to*
appeal *at*	appeal *to*
believe *at*	believe *in*
different *to*	different *from*
for least, *for* most	*at* least, *at* most
refer *at*	refer *to*
relevant *with*	relevant *to*
similar *with*	similar *to*
subscribe *with*	subscribe *to*

D6 Word Order

The importance of word order varies from language to language. In English, word order is extremely important, contributing a good deal to the meaning of a sentence.

(1) Standard Word Order

Like Chinese, English is an "SVO" language, or one in which the most typical sentence pattern is "subject-verb-object." (Arabic, by contrast, is an example of a "VSO" language.) Deviation from the SVO pattern tends to confuse English speakers.

(2) Word Order in Questions

Word order in questions can be particularly troublesome for speakers of languages other than English, partly because there are so many different ways to form questions in English.

CLOSE-UP: WORD ORDER IN QUESTIONS

1. To create a yes/no question from a statement using the verb *to be*, simply invert the order of the subject and the verb:

continued on the following page

continued from the previous page

<u>Rasheem is</u> researching the depletion of the ozone layer.

<u>Is Rasheem</u> researching the depletion of the ozone layer?

2. To create a yes/no question from a statement using a verb other than *to be*, use a form of the auxiliary verb *do* before the sentence without inverting the subject and verb:

<u>Does</u> Rasheem want to research the depletion of the ozone layer?

<u>Do</u> Rasheem's friends want to help him with his research?

<u>Did</u> Rasheem's professors approve his research proposal?

3. A question can also be formed by adding a **tag question**—such as *won't he?* or *didn't I?*—to the end of a statement. If the verb of the main statement is *positive*, then the verb of the tag question is *negative*; if the verb of the main statement is *negative*, then the verb of the tag question is *positive*:

Rasheem <u>is</u> researching the depletion of the ozone layer, <u>isn't</u> he?

Rasheem <u>doesn't</u> intend to write his dissertation about the depletion of the ozone layer, <u>does</u> he?

4. To create a question asking for information, use **interrogative** words (*who, what, where, when, why, how*) and invert the order of the subject and verb (note that *who* functions as the subject of the question in which it appears):

<u>Who is</u> researching the depletion of the ozone layer?

<u>What is Rasheem</u> researching?

<u>Where is Rasheem</u> researching the depletion of the ozone layer?

soon to become

A Harcourt Higher Learning Company

Soon you will find Harcourt Brace's distinguished innovation, leadership, and support under a different name ... a new brand that continues our unsurpassed quality, service, and commitment to education.

We are combining the strengths of our college imprints into one worldwide brand: ◎Harcourt Our mission is to make learning accessible to anyone, anywhere, anytime—reinforcing our commitment to lifelong learning.

We'll soon be Harcourt College Publishers. Ask for us by name.

One Company
"Where Learning Comes to Life."

INDEX

Index

Index

Index

Index